Loders Ba

(Schoolboy Memories from the 1950s and Pictures from Even Earlier)

Written and Compiled

by

Bernard Paull

With help and advice from friends and family

Uploders (West) c1930 by Claud Hider

Dedicated to family and friends and all who have ever lived in this delightful West Dorset village.

Lower Loders c1905 by Bridport Photographer Potts

First Published 2019

ISBN 978-1-5272-4950-9

Printed and bound in Great Britain by
Book Printing UK
Remus House, Coltsfoot Drive, Woodston, Peterborough, PE2 9BF

Loders Back-Along

Contents

Introduction

For almost 40 years I have been collecting postcards and photographs of Loders. Our old family photographs were a good starting point. I have added to these by spending many hours trawling through the stocks of dealers at postcard fairs and browsing the internet.

In 2001 I gave my first public display, 'Loders - A Trip Down Memory Lane' at the new Loders Village Hall. The pictures were photographed on to 35mm slides and displayed using a slide projector. As always happens, and to some amusement, one or two were upside-down or back-to-front but overall the evening went well with much audience participation. After the show several people kindly allowed me to borrow and copy their pictures and add them to the collection for future use. Some are included in this book.

Since then I have given a few more presentations, the last in 2018 for the Loders' History Society. After each I have had similar offers which I have been pleased to accept and for which I am extremely grateful.

At my first display in 2001 I was asked "Why don't you write a book?". Over the years I have written up the collection getting much help mainly from those older than I am who grew up in the village. Sadly, not many are left now. My mother was particularly good. She named almost all of the folks in the old family pictures and dated them.

With the help of these old postcards and photographs we can look back at life and events from about 1900 to the end of the 1950s.

Whenever possible (with the help of others) people in the photographs and locations are named. No doubt, some will be wrong. If they are, please let me know. It will corrected in the reprint; if there is one!

The girls and ladies in the pictures have been named as they were when the photographs were taken. If they married later and their married name is known it is added in brackets. If they were married when the picture was taken their married name will be given. In a few cases if, for example, they grew up in the village or had connections with it, their maiden names will also be given.

The Title. For anyone unfamiliar with the local dialect "Back-along" simply means 'in the past' or 'some time ago'. For example, if the old folks were asked when an event had taken place they would reply "Ah, that were back-along".

Part I covers the years just after the Second World War. It is based on my own personal recollections and those of a few others who were around then. It recalls how life in the village was in the late 1940s and 1950s. Although things had changed since the early 1900s, many aspects of life were not dissimilar to how they were 50 years earlier.

Part II looks at the period from about 1900 to just after the end of the Second World War. We take a journey through the village from east to west passing through Uploders, Yondover and Lower Loders to look back to those times and events of yester-year. Most people would have worked in the village or very nearby. Life otherwise centred around the family, the church, the school, the 'Big Houses', social groups and activities and, of course, the pubs which were just drinking places; very different from the pubs of today.

Thanks and Appreciation

I would like to give my thanks and appreciation to all of those who helped me in any way. In particular the following who knowingly, and sometimes unknowingly, have helped me put this book together.

Keith Alner, Pat Bown (née Ascott), Annelie Burrell (Talbot), Jessie Barrett (née Crabb), Helen Doble (née Crabb), Paul Fuszard, Christine Harris, Arthur Hobbs, Clive Jeanes, Brian Stidwell, Alan Symes, Philip Symes, Chuck Willmott and the Late Mrs Bishop, Bill Budden, Marjorie Randall, Andrew Skeats, Derrick Skeats and Tony Yarde for the use of their pictures and postcards, their knowledge, information and general help and advice.

Elizabeth Gale for her encouragement and advice from the beginning, her comments on the numerous drafts and spotting the mistakes in them. Also, for her contribution on the Askerswell and District Young Farmers.

Tommy Burt, Adrian Crabb, Maurice Crabb, David Crabb, Peter and Eileen Fuszard, Bryan Hyde, David Gill, Clifford Pitcher, Horace Read, Robin and Helen Wells and the Late Arthur Crabb, Clive Crabb and Raymond Crabb for the information I picked up in conversations with them.

Colin Ballard and Steven Lincoln for their help and advice in getting this book to print, Colin Bowditch for his input on the North Devon Reds.

Margot Blackah for undertaking the final proof reading and her good and helpful advice.

The postcard dealers who have helped me in the search for 'anything from Loders' and anyone else who I may have overlooked.

My mother, Annie Paull, who gave me such a good start with the old family pictures and postcards and who diligently recorded details of the pictures on their backs and who was able to give me information on any cards I had obtained.

Finally, my wife Christine for her considerable patience while I was compiling the book. (It took far longer than I thought it would!) For her ongoing checking, comments and advice on the wording and content and keeping me at it when I would have preferred to be doing other things

PART I
Village Life in the 1950s

Village Life in the 1950s

Domestic Life

As a child anywhere within our reach was our playground; the fields, the roads and river. The only consideration was to arrive home in time for dinner! We wore our clothes until they were worn out. Our socks and jumpers were darned and patches sewn on our trousers and jackets. The older generation were addressed as Mr, Mrs or Miss unless they were relations. Many were, in which case they were uncle, aunty, granny or grandad. Our mothers wore frocks, we listened to the wireless, couples went courting and we caught the train at the *RAILWAY* Station! (Where did *Train Station* come from?)

Most of the families in the village could be traced back generations. Although the numbers working on the farms had dwindled with the introduction of mechanisation a lot were still employed as farmworkers. There were many small farms run by the husband and wife with occasional help from casual labour. A few men specialised in this type of work and did a bit of hedging and ditching or helped at harvest and other busy times. Others worked in Bridport or in other nearby villages. The houses were permanently occupied by these local working families, their elderly relatives and a few who had moved in for retirement. There were no holiday lettings or second homes.

The domestic arrangements were very simple and straightforward. When first married most women carried on working. Once the children came along they took on a different role. They stayed at home to look after the family, to cook, wash, iron, clean, tend to any livestock they might have and to keep the flower garden (or the flower knot as it was called then) colourful, neat and tidy.

They also took responsibility for elderly relatives who either lived with them or somewhere close by. The elderly couples stayed in their houses as long as they were able but once one of them passed away it was not unusual that the surviving one moved in with the family. There was very little social care as we know it and although there were Homes for the elderly and infirm they were firmly resisted by anyone approaching that time of life. "I will never go into a Home" were words we had all heard and understood. Who would want to?

The men went to work for five and a half or even six days a week for long hours and with overtime when demanded. They tended the garden, not as a hobby but as a necessity, to supply fruit and vegetables for the family. They did repairs and decorating around the house and occasionally went to the pub for a couple of pints.

To fill in any spare time they might have and to earn a bit of extra money a lot of the women in and around Bridport, including Loders, took in work from the Bridport net firms. Annie Paull, my mother (left) was one of them. Here she is in the garden, braiding on a warm and sunny summer evening.

We ate vegetables in season and looked forward to the first pickings of peas, broad beans, runner beans, potatoes, carrots, strawberries and raspberries but maybe not so much the Brussels sprouts!

People grew a lot of their own produce but there were still a couple of market gardeners. I remember my mother buying new potatoes from Sid Marsh at 37, Loders. He had wonderful crops in a well stocked garden that stretched from the back of his cottage down to the river.

Domestic freezers had not yet arrived in Loders so fruit and vegetables were preserved in other ways. Fruit was bottled or used to make jam. Apples were carefully wrapped in paper and stored in cool houses alongside potatoes in wooden boxes and onions on strings. Runner beans were sliced and placed in jars in layers with salt in between for use over the winter. Removed from the jars, thoroughly rinsed then cooked, they tended to taste salty but were fine. A taste of summer in the winter.

Even though much of the war-time rationing had ended supplies in the shops were limited compared with today so very little was wasted. We ate (or were expected to eat) all of the food on our plates. We had fruit and vegetables from the garden and many kept chickens but if not, eggs were readily available from farms or from people who kept poultry.

Frank and Ena Crabb, our next door neighbours and my uncle and aunt, kept chickens and occasionally geese for the oven at Christmas. They had a big chicken run with a couple of hutches and fresh spring water that trickled from a pipe into a large metal bowl. The bowl was similar to that in an old copper; more details of that later. Foxes were always a threat to chickens but with Uncle Frank's secure fence there were never any problems.

The chickens were well fed with corn and maize. They were also given a mix of bran with potato peelings, stale bread and any other vegetable waste but no meat, all mixed together and cooked.

I rather liked the aroma that came from the stodgy mix as it cooked. The smell was similar to that from the brewery when they are brewing which I also enjoy! The chickens enjoyed it too and tucked in to the sticky mix in the trough.

At the back of Frank and Ena's house there was a glass lean-to which, up to about 1950-ish, had a large glazed earthenware jar containing preserved eggs in a mysterious solution. Having researched the subject, the preservative would have been Isinglass or, probably, Water-Glass. The Water-Glass came as a powder in a tin.

The powder was poured into a bucket and mixed with water until it reached the right consistency like a very liquid wallpaper paste and cloudy grey in colour. Any surplus eggs were lowered gently into the jar and covered with the Water-Glass mix.

How long the eggs remained edible I do not know but I imagine they were marked with the date they were laid to ensure that the older ones were used first. To my knowledge I never had the pleasure of eating one. Or maybe I was just not told!

Electricity

Electricity arrived in 1936. By 1950 most houses had been connected. Electricians Edward Marsh from Trossachs (now Butterwell) and Maurice Tucker, the son of Henry Tucker the head gardener at Uploders House, wired many village properties.

People enjoyed the pleasure and convenience of light at the flick of a switch and the ease and cleanliness of cooking on an electric cooker, (above right) compared with the kitchen range (left). Most agreed, though, that food cooked in the range tasted much better and the meat was more tender than when cooked in the electric oven. I would not disagree but electricity did make life a great deal easier!

My Great-grandfather's brother Alf Marsh and his wife Emily moved from Maycroft Road, Weymouth to Maycroft in Uploders when he retired from the Police. This probably explains why the house is named 'Maycroft', or perhaps it was just a coincidence. The rented house had no electricity and it remained that way until Emily passed away in about 1970. She was widowed in 1947 and although the landlord offered to install electricity she preferred to carry on as she always had with coal fires, oil lamps and the range. Maycroft was probably the last house in the village not to have mains electricity.

The Wireless

The wireless (left) gave us the BBC Light Programme and Home Service and programmes we would not miss; The Archers, Dick Barton Special Agent, Journey in to Space, Life with the Lyons, Have-a-Go with Wilfred Pickles, Family Favourites on Sundays and many others.

In the evenings we tried to tune in to Radio Luxembourg (on 208 metres medium wave band) to listen to the latest pop music. Being a commercial station there were the adverts. We all remember the Infra-Draw method devised by Horace Batchelor from Keynsham (spelt K-E-Y-N-S-H-A-M,) Bristol which guaranteed wins on the football pools. If the method was that good, I wondered, why didn't he just keep it to himself?

Even though there was mains electricity after 1936 a few of the more elderly folk still kept their old wireless set that ran on an accumulator (right). This was similar to a car battery with lead plates and sulphuric acid in a thick glass container. The accumulators, like any battery, went flat with use but could be recharged.

Mr Brown at Brook Barton offered a re-charging service in the 1950s. Ackerman's from Bridport offered a similar service but this was probably before mains electricity was installed. They visited the village weekly and replaced discharged accumulators with fully charged ones. To make sure they always had a charged accumulator people had several on standby.

Water Supply

Mains water came along in 1963. Prior to that people managed without any problem. It was what we were used to. Every property had access to its own or a shared well or water chute. I can recall two drinking water chutes. In Uploders the water came from an iron pipe in the wall of Pine Cottages, (Tiddly Cottage) into the drain on the roadside. The pipe is still there but no water. The spring that fed it was probably diverted by the construction of the foundations for the garage built a few years ago.

Yondover has two chutes. The one closest to Uploders on the south side of the road was drinking water. It was collected in buckets and carried back to the nearby houses for drinking and washing. On the way home from school on hot days we would cup our hand under the cool, fresh water and have a few mouthfuls to keep us going until we arrived home. Marjorie Randall told me that her mother used to scrub the chute every fortnight so that it was always spotlessly clean. I can confirm that this was most definitely the case! The water from the lower chute was, and still is, not suitable for drinking.

Water from shallow wells was dipped out with buckets. Deeper wells had a hand-pump alongside. During the 1950s and before the mains came along most properties had running water indoors. In our case a Stuart Turner pump pumped the water from the well to a tank in the roof which fed a tap in the kitchen. As the water level in the tank dropped the float switch triggered the pump and stopped it when the water reached a pre-determined level. The Bradpole plumber George Turner installed ours and many others in the village.

Our well (right) was shallow with half a dozen steps leading down to the water. It had a stone slab half-roof opposite the steps which gave some protection but it was effectively open to the atmosphere. Alf Hallett, my Godfather was an inspector with the local board and was very unhappy that we, and the rest of the inhabitants of Loders, were drinking untested and untreated water. I'm not certain if he ever drank any but I do know that he was a lot happier when we were connected to the mains supply.

As far as I know none of the village folk suffered any ill effects from drinking our untested and untreated water. We probably built up an immunity to any nasties. Or maybe it was bred in to our genes!

Rain-water was collected in butts, tanks and barrels for a number of domestic and personal uses. Our cat Mickey sitting on the rain water tank (left) - a favourite position as it caught the morning sun.

In this limestone area the groundwater is naturally hard and does not lather well. Rainwater gathered in the water butts is soft and was much preferred by the ladies for their personal hygiene; the daily strip wash, a bath, and particularly for washing their hair. The men were not so particular and used any water, probably with carbolic soap!

The Monday washing also benefitted from the use of the soft rain-water. Less soap was needed and there was a lot less scum around the copper at the end of the washing.

Bath time was a fairly major undertaking. It was usual to have a bath once a week whether it was needed or not! Usually it was on a Sunday before school the next day. The water was heated in a copper or an electric boiler and transferred to a tin bath. Our Belling boiler was easy, simply turn on the tap and run the water into the bath. With a copper the water was transferred to the bath using a bowl-dipper (right) a small metal bowl with a wooden handle. On other days the folks washed thoroughly using a bowl of hot water, soap and a flannel. Showers had not yet arrived in Loders, or many other rural places for that matter.

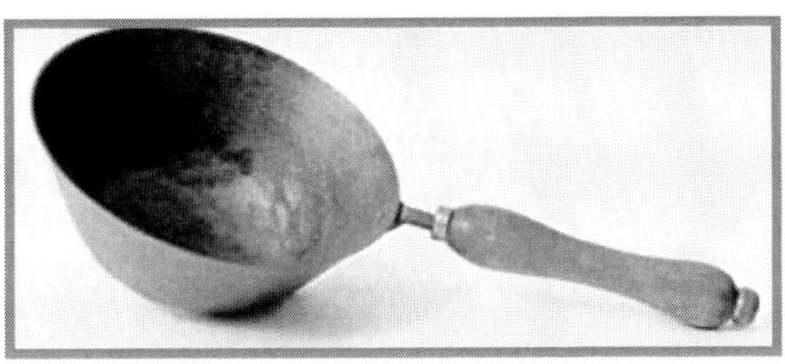

Looking back it all sounds very primitive but the people, their clothes and houses were clean and well looked after. Compared with how life was 50 years earlier, life in Loders in the 1950s had made a big step forward.

Monday was Washing Day

Bonfires on a Monday were strictly taboo!

Most houses had a wash-house. The one (above left) was at West View (Killick Cottage). It, like many others originally had a copper (above, right). This was a semi-spherical bowl, made from iron not copper, about 18 inches (450mm) in diameter. It was built into a brickwork or stone fireplace. On washing day the bowl was filled with water by bucket and the fire under the bowl lit to heat the water. A wooden lid kept the heat in.

The whites with added soapflakes were put into the copper and the water heated to boiling point. All the time the contents were prodded and stirred with a wooden washing dolly bleached white with use. After some time, the whites were removed with wooden tongs and rinsed in a galvanised tin bath filled with cold water. A blue-bag was added to give that extra special sparkle to the whites.

If needed some of the hot water was baled out with a 'bowl-dipper' and used to wash small items. The remaining water that had already been used to wash the whites was then used for the coloured items.

During the early 1950s most of the old coppers were replaced with electric boilers and later twin-tub washing machines. Life became easier.

After rinsing, the washing was put through the mangle, or ringer (right), to squeeze out the water. This involved feeding one end of the washing between the rollers and then turning the handle. As the item of washing was squeezed between the rollers the water poured out and was collected in a bowl that was placed on the platform beneath the rollers.

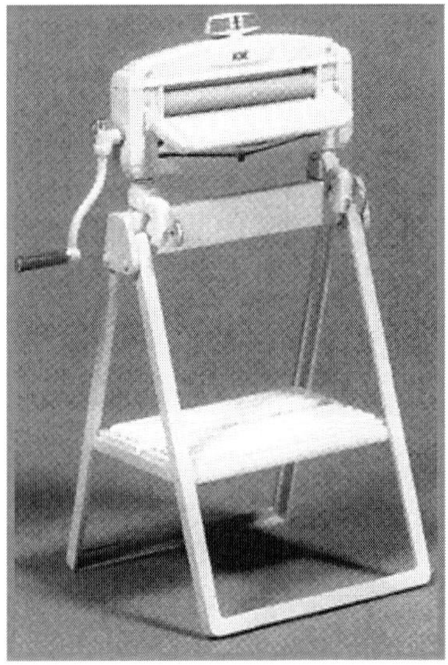

The mangle was a very effective and efficient piece of equipment and good fun to use. It was one of the domestic chores that we were willing to help with without too much complaint!

The rollers were spring-loaded so the pressure on any particular item could be adjusted. For sheets, towels and similar the screw on the top would be tightened so that the maximum amount of water came out. For items with buttons the springs were loosened because if the rollers were too tight there was a good chance that the buttons would be broken.

The washing then went on to the washing line, having first of all checked to make sure there were no rogue bonfires. Woe-betide anyone who had started a bonfire.

The final step was the ironing. By the 1950s almost everyone had an electric iron so it was just a case of plug it in and switch it on. If there was no wall socket the iron was plugged into the light socket. My grandmother had a two-way adaptor in the light socket which held the light bulb with a spare connection at the side for her iron. She never had a problem with it which I find surprising!

Prior to the electric iron, flat-irons (left) were used generally in pairs. They were warmed in front of the fire, on top of the range or in the oven. When the first iron was being used the second was warming ready for when the first one had cooled. Some folks kept their old flat irons for ornamental purposes but, if there happened to be a power cut, they came in very handy.

Toilet Facilities

There were no main sewers in the village until 1972-73. In the 1950s a few properties had the luxury of a flush toilet discharging into a septic tank and. I have it on good authority, directly in to the river. The vast majority did not. They had a more primitive earth closet or Elsan lavatory (lavvy or privy were the polite other names). They were situated in a far-flung corner of the garden; presumably for reasons of hygiene. In other villages, Netherbury, Broadwindsor and Abbotsbury and no doubt, many others, some were built directly above a stream which gave a convenient, efficient but not particularly hygienic system of sewage disposal.

They had no windows so were dark with spiders but were spotlessly clean. In frosty weather they were cold so visits were quick. No sitting around reading a comic or newspaper! One of the hazards of making a visit on a dark wet evening was the possibility (quite a high one) of stepping on some poor unsuspecting slugs and snails that were going about their business on the garden path. Not nice!

At Shatcombe House (left) the toilet was tucked away in a far corner of the garden. It had a change of use in 1973 when it became a garden tool shed. The building with a tiled roof was Willow Cottage's privy. The building with the brick corner (on the right) was the wash-house with a copper.

The lavatory designs varied. Trossachs (Butterwell) in Uploders had a two-seater and one of the cottages in Yondover a three-seater. The three-seater was about twice the width of the normal. It had a well scrubbed wooden seat which extended the full width of the building. If I remember correctly, the openings at the seating positions were small, medium and large. The three bears always came to mind when I paid a visit!

In 1973 virtually every property was connected to the main sewer. New indoor toilets were installed and small bedrooms and box-rooms converted to bathrooms. The impact of the sewers was far greater than the arrival of the water mains. Then it was just different water flowing from the same tap. The sewer took life into the 20th century.

Transport

Very few people had cars but the Southern National Bus Company ran an excellent service with its green and cream buses. The route was Bridport to Askerswell and back. A workman's bus left Uploders for Bridport at about seven-thirty in the morning. A bus for shoppers left at ten-to-ten and returned at one o'clock. This bus went on to Askerswell, turned and picked up in Uploders at half-past-one. The next bus from Bridport was at four-thirty with another service for the workmen leaving Bridport at about quarter-past-six, after the net factories closed at six.

On Saturdays a late bus left Bridport at about quarter-to-nine in the evening. This fitted in neatly with going to the pictures at the Palace and the Lyric. They both ran two sittings, or houses, made up of the supporting film, Pathé News (left), the main film and at the end the National Anthem when the audience stood to attention and sang the words. The bus timetable was such that we went for the start of the main film of the first house and left at the end of the supporting film at the second house. The National Anthem came in the middle.

Most of our fathers worked in Bridport and usually cycled to work. If the weather was bad they might catch the workmen's bus but the weather had to be really bad for this to happen. Most started work at eight o'clock so several of them, my father included, set out together at just after half-past-seven to make a leisurely and sociable journey to work. Today it would probably be a 'commute' to work. To we folks in the country commuters only existed in London. The men took a pack of sandwiches wrapped in grease-proof paper and some took a thermos generally with tea. There were no take-away coffees in those days!

As far as we youngsters were concerned we made most of our journeys on our bikes. Even if it was only 50 yards down the road to one of our mates' homes or to Bridport, West Bay, Burton Bradstock and the adjacent villages. Between us we had a few elderly relatives conveniently scattered around who we could visit particularly if we were in need of refreshment, which we invariably were. They always made us welcome and we received a pat on the head when we reported back home that we had called to see them.

To go longer distances we went by bus or train. To anyone living in and around Bridport public transport was much better then than it is today. To get to London was simple, catch the train at Bridport Station (right), change at Maiden Newton to join the Weymouth to Paddington train.

Maiden Newton was the gateway to almost anywhere in the country. The north-bound line led to the Midlands, the North and South Wales via Bristol, to the West Country and to London (Paddington). The south-bound line took us to Dorchester and Weymouth with a connection to the Weymouth–Waterloo line at Dorchester. For destinations on this line including, for example, Bournemouth, passengers from Bridport changed at Maiden Newton, took the south-bound train to Weymouth, alighted at Dorchester West, walked to Dorchester South and boarded the Weymouth to Waterloo train which stopped at Bournemouth as well as every station on the way!

There was serious talk of a railway halt at Loders but sadly it never happened and even sadder was the closure of the Bridport to Maiden Newton branch line in May 1975. At the time it was inevitable as it carried hardly any passengers but, were it still here, maybe it would be well used again. We will never know.

The Royal Blue coach company ran a fast and efficient coach service along the South Coast. Bridport Coach Station was a stopping point that connected with other services and was a comfort stop for the passengers. This made it very easy for people from this area to catch the Royal Blue. The routes ran between Penzance and London so were convenient for many destinations along the south coast or further afield with a change of coach.

The Black & White Bus Company of Cheltenham ran a service between Cheltenham and Bridport which linked up with the Royal Blue east-west route. It also provided a good link for north-bound travellers from Bridport. We had relatives in Cheltenham who originated from Loders. This coach service was very handy for them to return here and for us to visit them

Shopping and Tradesmen

In the early 1900s the village had carpenters, thatchers, blacksmiths, a cobbler, builders and carriers. There was a butcher, a post office and small shops. Local bakers delivered bread and farmers the milk. Many folk kept chickens for eggs or they could be bought from the farms.

In the 1950s there were still several small businesses in Uploders that made life easier for people. Grannie Hyde ran a shop from her house, Riverdale, selling tinned food, jams and marmalade, Lyons cakes, Smith's crisps, blocks of salt and many other delicacies. There was great excitement on 5 February 1953 when sweet rationing ended. Grannie Hyde gave us advance notice that sweets would be on sale on that day. Nationally as well as locally stocks quickly ran out and rationing returned!

At 2 Box Cottages Walter Tudball, the cobbler, worked from his front-room which was dedicated to shoe repairs. He moved to Uploders in 1932 and retired in 1952 aged 84 having spent 68 years as a cobbler. He worked at a table in a room with walls and ceiling blackened from years of coal fires and oil lamps. He was surrounded by the tools of his trade, piles of leather, nails, hob-nails (for boots), Blakey's protectors and all the other bits and pieces associated with his trade. An oilskin cloth covered his table. At meal times he cleared a patch and laid a sheet of newspaper as a tablecloth. At the end of his meal he screwed up the paper and, in the winter, used it to light the fire the next day. He worked six days a week. On a Saturday evening he put everything away in readiness for his day of rest on the Sabbath. He regularly attended the Methodist Chapel across the road. Mr Tudball (above, left) on a workday, and right, in his Sunday best ready for Chapel.

There was Charlie Gale the blacksmith and Mr Brown who did contracting work, road repairs and the like, and recharged acid batteries. Both are mentioned elsewhere.

Lower Loders had the village post office, shop and butchers. Mrs Wells ran the shop and post office. Albert (Tubby) Wells, her husband, was the butcher with a slaughterhouse behind their house and the post office.

The village was served by at least three Bridport grocers. Pearks' Stores ran a large green bus-like vehicle with no windows along the sides. It was lined with shelves and had a fold-down counter at the back where Mr Reeves served his customers. When Pearks' closed, Mr Reeves ran a small grocer's shop on the east side of the road towards the bottom end of South Street in Bridport.

Other grocers, International Stores, Cornick's, Whitemore's and Elliot's did it differently. During the week the delivery man called with his order book. He sat at the table and took the order for the week's groceries from his customer and then delivered it a few days later. The Elliot's order and delivery man was Joe Jeanes. He drove a brown 'Elliot's' van CFX 640. He was also a keen local politician, a member of Bridport Town Council and was Mayor twice; in 1981 and 1983. He is pictured in Part II with the delivery van and staff of Elliott's in about 1930.

Bread was delivered several days a week. It came fresh and still warm from the ovens. There was nothing more enjoyable than a hot crust with a generous spread of what quickly became melted butter and cheese! Caddy's from Bradpole who took over from Corbin's and also ran Bradpole Post Office made and delivered bread. Also, Roberts, Samways (with a green van) and the Co-op from Bridport. Pictured above are Whitemore's and Roberts' delivery vans parked in South Street, Bridport.

Newspapers were delivered Monday to Saturday by Cyril Tiltman who also ran the St Andrew's Road Post Office. Almost everyone had a newspaper so it was a busy round but Cyril was so quick that it was no problem for him. The Echo was delivered in the evenings usually by a school-boy earning a bit of pocket-money. A Mr Lee delivered the Sunday papers.

We had mail deliveries twice a day; early morning and afternoon. People knew that a letter posted in time to catch the first collection at the post-box would be delivered in Bridport and surrounding villages that afternoon. It was not unusual to send a postcard with the message "See you for tea this afternoon". All of this with flat rate postal service, no first and second class mail.

Paraffin and household hardware items were supplied by Mr Major and Bazley's but the one I recall the best is Mr Fuszard who delivered on Saturday afternoons often with his sons Peter and John. He wore a grey warehouse coat and a trilby hat. Captain Mainwaring of Dad's Army reminds me of him. The picture (inset) was taken in December 1949. He sold paraffin for lamps, heaters and stoves, soap (mainly of the carbolic type), brushes, buckets, bowls, saucepans clothes' pegs and all manner of similar useful household items from the back of his Bedford van. He also repaired saucepans and other household items. Many years later I was lucky enough to work with his grandson, Paul. One of the first things I mentioned when we first met was that I remembered his grandad. He was not surprised as it seems that almost everyone of a certain age from Bridport and around remembers his grandad. He would have been more surprised if I hadn't!

Milk came in electric milk floats to the doorstep six days a week in pint and half pint bottles from Rax Dairy. Percy Norfolk, the owner, was a member of Bridport Town Council for many years and was Mayor seven times between 1970 and 1980.

Rax Dairy operated from a shop in East Street (above) which besides milk and other dairy products had a café at the back and sold its own brand of very delicious ice-cream.

Meat was rationed until 1954 so a rabbit was always welcome. They were pests to the farmers so the rabbit-catchers were always in demand. We sometimes went with them to 'help'. Nets were placed at the mouth of the burrows and a ferret popped in. Fairly quickly there would be a bit of a commotion and a rabbit would come flying out only to tangle in the net. The rabbit catcher then stepped in, did what was necessary while we looked on wide-eyed! The rabbits were paunched (gutted), one back leg split open and the other slipped through to create a loop so that they could be easily carried on a stick or pole. They went to the butchers as well as the locals and, of course, the 'helpers' had a share.

When there was a good catch of mackerel the fishermen from Abbotsbury, Burton Bradstock and West Bay would go around the villages selling their catch. They did a roaring trade and the fresh mackerel made a lovely tasty supper!

Coal came in wagons by goods trains to Bridport Station where Bradford's had a dêpot. It was collected from the station by other coal merchants and taken to their yards for bagging. It was then delivered to customers around the area. In Loders it arrived on the same day every two weeks in one-hundred-weight bags (51kg) carried on the coalman's back, in some cases up long garden paths. Ours came courtesy of two of the Cox brothers, Ralf and Bimbo.

Men of the 1950s and earlier did not shop if they could avoid it. My father was one of them. If he needed (note, needed not wanted) a new pair of trousers my mother went to Snook's in Bridport and brought home two or three pairs on 'appro' (approval). The unwanted trousers were returned and the chosen pair paid for. My mother who worked in Day's and Elmes's when she left school told of the ladies who went in to the shop on a Friday for two or three hats on appro only to return all of them on the Monday as being unsuitable. This seemed to happen more when there was a wedding or some important civic event over the weekend!

Wally Stoodley, from Powerstock sold items of clothing and linen which were ordered from his catalogue and paid for at so much a week. Philip Symes recalls that in the 1930s Reece's shoe shop also delivered shoes which were paid for in the same way. The purchaser was issued with a personal book in which the debt and repayments were recorded.

Wally also collected coupons for football pools entries; Littlewoods, Vernon's, Zetters etc. His customers lived in hope of winning the magic jackpot of £75,000!

School

I was due to start school after Easter in 1949 but Miss Wilkes, the Head Mistress and only teacher, (right, as she was in 1928) suggested that as I was the only starter it would be better to wait until after the summer holidays when four others were due to join the school. So, on 30 August 1949 Janet Bond, Terrence Symes, Mary and Rosamond, the Willmott twins and I joined the other 20, or so, pupils at Loders School where I remained until July 1955.

The main entrance then was through the front porch off the road, traffic was no worry then. The classroom area stretched the whole length of the road side of the school. It could be divided in two with a sliding wooden glazed partition. The south wing was the dining area and was used for PE in wet weather, exercises and the like. There were two age groups, Infants and Juniors. Presumably there were Seniors when the school took pupils up to 14 years of age.

The Juniors occupied the east end of the school and sat in rows of flip-top desks with an ink-well in the corner (above). The infants were at the west end. One teacher taught children from 5 to 11 years old. No easy task but we all left school able to read, write and do arithmetic and a good proportion passed the 11-Plus exams and went on to study at Bridport Grammar School.

The school was heated by three coke stoves (right), The front class-room area had one in the north-east corner and one in the north-west corner. The third was halfway along the wall of the dining area. The fires were lit before school by the caretaker, Mrs Darby or Mrs Chard for much of the time I was there. Each stove had a coke hod for topping-up. It was a large space to be heated by three stoves so good thick woolly jumpers were needed in the winter months.

The coke and faggots for fire lighting were stored in a galvanised iron lean-to in the playground at the east end of the main building.

All school children received milk at school. It came in ⅓ pint bottles with a cardboard top. The tops had a hole half-punched in the middle so that a careful pressing made a hole for the straw (paper not plastic!). Careless or clumsy pressing, on the other hand, created a spurt of milk, a mess on the floor and a good ticking off.

The milk was delivered to the front door early in the morning so that in frosty weather it was partially frozen. The crates were stacked by the stoves to thaw out the milk. By break time the bottles nearest the stove were warm. I was not keen on milk and even less keen on warm milk so I always made a dash to make sure I got one of the chilly and probably still partially frozen bottles. I'm sure the milk did us a power of good!

Our school dinners were delivered in aluminium containers by Mr Trent in his brown warehouse coat. The meals were served by our kindly dinner ladies. I remember Mrs Darby and later Mrs Chard and Mrs Dora Legg. I have hazy memories of stalky cabbage, black hard bits in the potatoes, stringy meat, and semolina, custard and gravy, all of the lumpy variety. Then there was the bad news; mince. It came in a cylindrical insulated container and, if you were near the front of the queue you saw what was inside when the lid was removed. A three inch layer of grease which the dinner ladies stirred in to the mix with a large ladle no doubt hoping that we had not seen it but we had! Having said that, at the end of a long morning we were hungry so although we moaned about it we tucked in and even enjoyed it.. Treacle-sponge with custard drew few complaints even if the custard happened to be a bit lumpy. Best of all was the chocolate-sponge with chocolate sauce!

In 1949 a stone wall divided the playground in two. Looking towards Boarsbarrow Hill the big boys were on the left, the girls and first year boys on the right. The segregating wall was eventually demolished so that the boys and girls played together.

In 1951 hot and cold running water was installed, pumped from the well in the playground and chlorinated. The toilets were at the bottom of the playground and in 1949 were of the earth closet type. They would have remained like that at least until the running water was provided in 1951 .

Martha Crabb lived in the thatched cottage next to the school with just a stone wall between her garden and the playground. Balls often ended up in her garden but she didn't mind. She returned them with a smile and a few words. She was a lovely old lady known to us all as Aunt Martha.

Miss Wilkes joined Loders School in 1927, possibly as head teacher. She was definitely head in 1929. Below is an extract from Annie Hawker's (my mother) report of Christmas 1929. It is countersigned by Annie's mother Emily Hawker; my grandmother

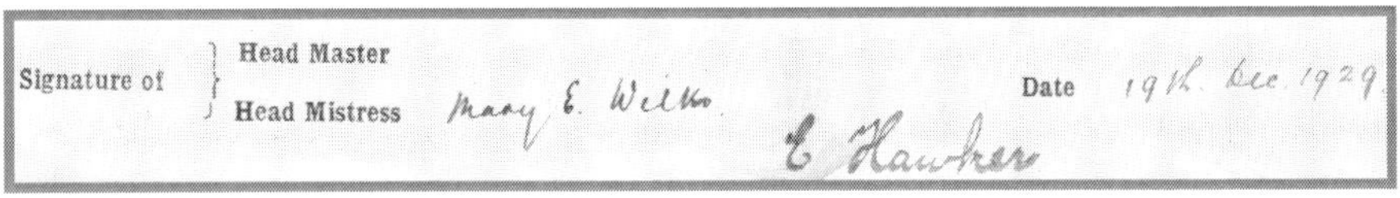

Signature of Head Master / Head Mistress Mary E. Wilks

Date 19th. Dec. 1929

E Hawker

Miss Wilkes retired in July 1950 having spent 23 years most, if not all, of which she was the Headmistress.

Miss Barlow became head and only teacher when Miss Wilkes retired in 1950. (Below) The school in 1951 with Miss Barlow and the 21 pupils,

(Back row) Miss Barlow, Reggie Drake, Morwenna Willmott, Caroline Elliott, Graham Legg, Tony Yarde, Margaret Drake and Ruth Willmott.
(Middle row) Janet Bond, Pauline Dunkerton, Bernard Paull, Jennifer Paul, Richard Elliott, Alan Wheeler and Pauline Legg.
(Front row) Rosamond Willmott, Mary Willmott, Brian Harper, David Skeats, Terence Symes, Maureen Crabb and Kenny Drake.

As the pupil numbers increased slightly the authorities were persuaded to provide a second teacher and so Miss Wickham joined the school in September 1951. She taught the seniors leaving Miss Barlow, or Mrs Clark as she became, to teach the infants. Mrs Clark left in July 1952 after two years in charge and was replaced by Miss Barbara Bryan.

On 23 August 2018 a picture of the Loders School Children in 1954 was published in the Bridport News. It was sent in by Mrs Joan Ellis, née Laramy, who taught at the school for a term in 1954 before she left for Teacher Training College. The headteacher at the time was Miss Barbara Bryan. She was the sole teacher until Miss Laramy joined her for a term.

Joan asked if anyone could name the pupils. Several of us, mainly ex-pupils, contacted her, each other and the Bridport News. Between us we managed to name everyone, we hope correctly. The article from the Bridport News is reproduced on the next page.
Miss Laramy and the pupils.
(Back row) David Skeats, Alan Wheeler, Brian Bolton, Bernard Paull, Richard Elliot, Kenneth Brown.
(One row from back) Lynette Driver, Bryan Hyde, Terrence Symes, Mary Willmott, Evelyn Elliot. Annabel Howell, Jennifer Coombe, Rosamund Willmott, Maureen Crabb.
(Kneeling) Tommy Dennett, Janette Bolton, Eddie Edrich, David Gill, Dan Elliot, Mervyn Legg.
(Front row) Vivien Legg, Juliet Willmott, Terry Linee, Miss Laramy, Christopher Coombe, Susan Elliot, Christine Bunnell, Annelie Burrell.

Article from the Bridport News on 23 August 2018

Can you spot anyone in class?

WE are helping a former student teacher to remind an ex-class of their childhood days.

An ex-student teacher, who spent the summer term at Loders School, is hoping that through sharing some old photographs of the class, that readers may recognise one or two old faces.

Joan Ellison (nee Laramy) has provided some information and pictures to the Bridport News for this piece, and was at the school in 1954, before attending Teacher Training College, and enjoyed her time at the school.

Joan said: "These photos show all the pupils with Miss Bryan, the headteacher, the same group with me and then the infants with whom I worked with.

"Miss Bryan was the sole teacher and she worked very hard, and was very caring, and especially helpful to me."

On the day of Joan's arrival at the school in April 1954, it had snow quite heavily, and she walked to the village from the main Beaminster to Bridport Road, and on arrival found the Vicar and a small number of children.

Joan said: "The Vicar informed me that I had to take the children to church for a short service for beginning of term.

"No other pupils arrived and neither did Miss Bryan so the children took me to the church.

"We then returned to the classroom and enjoyed chatting about this until eventually, Miss Bryan was able to get through the snow to school."

From that point on, Joan was advised each day what to do with her little class, who she commented were 'all delightful and so enjoyable'.

Joan said: "They really were lovely and well behaved and fun to be with."

Joan told the Bridport News that some of her ex-students remain firmly in her mind, in particular the boys, who were keen on their games, and the son of the local policeman, who was the most mischievous of the lot.

She said: "One who was a farmer's son, told me very firmly that the 'cows' I spoke about on a nature walk, were not cows at all but were 'heifers'.

"I can hear his Dorset accent now."

Joan also commented that the girls were all charming and giggly, especially the Vicar's daughter, who she said: "Was very pretty and always smiling."

Joan is hoping that through her pictures, some of her ex-pupils will recognise themselves and rekindle those childhood memories.

Joan said: "It was a very happy little school and I have many happy memories of my time there."

If you would like to get in contact with Joan, you can email news@bridportnews.co.uk and we will forward your details on.

Miss Laramy's class, the infants, Summer Term 1954.
(Back) David Gill, Juliet Willmott, Eddie Edrich, Janette Bolton, Tommy Dennett, Lynette Driver.
(Middle) Terry Linee, Annelie Burrell, Christopher Coombe, Susan Elliot.
(Front) Vivien Legg, Christine Bunnell.

Right, the Head Teacher, Miss Barbara Bryan, who drove to school each day from nearby Askerswell where she lived. There was much excitement when she changed her car to a new Morris Minor registration number NGU 882. As a pupil I thought she was fairly elderly but looking at her picture now she looks remarkably young!

Sadly Miss Laramy left us at the end of the summer term. Below is an extract from the Reverend Oliver Willmott's Parish Notes which describes the leaving ceremony far, far better than I could even if I had remembered.

"Miss Barbara Bryan initiated a parents' day at Loders School with great success. Parents and school managers in large number turned up to inspect the children's exercise books, and specimens of handwork which adorned the walls. The infants then presented a fairy dance, and the juniors a play. Miss Laramy, the probation teacher who has been helping Miss Bryan, leaves this term for Weymouth College. On behalf of the parents of the Infants, Terence Linee presented her with an equipped sponge bag, and Linette Driver with an alarm clock. Mrs Willmott spoke of the regard that parents and children felt at Miss Laramy's departure. Alan Wheeler then presented Miss Bryan with a box of chocolates to the applause of the school."

Miss Bryan is the teacher I remember most clearly, probably because she was head for the last three years of my six years at Loders School. She came from a large school in Blandford and during the War she had an important role at the Signals' Department of Sir Winston Churchill's underground Headquarters in Whitehall. She was an excellent teacher who carried on the good work of those before her. She was strict but treated us all very fairly. She married in August 1955 about a month after I left Loders School for Bridport Grammar School.

In our final year and being the oldest pupils we were given extra jobs and responsibilities. One I enjoyed was popping to Mrs May Wells's post office and shop to buy stamps and stationery items. Amongst many other things, the shop stocked economy labels for the re-use of second-hand envelopes. Ten years after the end of the war there was still a shortage of many everyday items. The labels were used to cover the addresses and reseal the old envelopes. We would call it recycling. As children we were slightly nervous of Mrs Wells, the Post Mistress. She stood no nonsense but as long as we behaved properly she treated us like adults. As I was on a lone mission with errands from school it was difficult to do anything other than behave properly so we got on handsomely.

Like all children we were quick to learn the things it would have been better not to have learnt. A couple of local builders were carrying out repairs on the school. This was something different so at playtime we gathered round their ladder to watch, ask a lot of questions, poke around their tools and materials and make a general nuisance of ourselves.

The builders soon grew tired of this. So, for a bit of peace and quiet for them and for our safety they told us in no uncertain terms what we understood to mean "get lost or go away". The instruction was clear but it was given using a strange new word which I later discovered was of Anglo -Saxon origins. This new expression and the way that it was put to us made a big impression on us so we spent much of the rest of playtime mimicking the builders and telling each other to "****-off". We were canny enough to realise that it would be unwise to say this in front of teacher; but we did not forget.

As usual our mothers collected us after school and as we ambled back home we began to tell each other to "****-off" in the same way our builder friends had told us to. Looks of horror appeared on our mothers faces. Mine got hold of me and with an extremely severe look on her face said "Don't you ***EVER*** let me hear you say that word again!!". I can confirm that she never did, the look on her face convinced me that she really did mean it!

Leisure Time

There were no playgrounds or parks. The whole of the area was our playground; the fields, the lanes, the woods and, best of all, the rivers and streams. We made camps in the hedgerows and woods, played football and cricket on the fields that were reasonably flat and tried to build dams across the Asker. The farmers didn't mind as long as we caused no damage which generally we didn't. Most of what we did meant that we returned home muddy or wet through. The muckier we were the happier we were; but not our mothers.

There were so few cars that we could ride on go-carts, play cricket and football on the road without any serious interruption. For cricket we used a Corona fizzy drinks box as a wicket. At the start we played our shots straight back or past the bowler but we soon had a rush of blood so the ball inevitably ended up in front gardens and through open front doors. Most people remembered that they were young once and were happy for us to retrieve the ball. There was one exception who called the police on more than one occasion. We got a gentle and understanding lecture from the village bobby and then got back to the game.

The girls played hop-scotch. We occasionally joined in but not too often. It wasn't good to be seen playing girls' games by any school mates that might pass by and, not only that, the girls were better than the boys!

In wet weather we went to each other's houses to play cards and games. None of us had learnt to be good losers so games like Monopoly where defeat is like a lingering, painful death usually ended with a smirking winner and tantrums from the losers.

When we were about 11 or 12 years old one of our pastimes was collecting car numbers. We cycled up New Road to Loders Cross on the A35 and sat on the boundary wall of Gribb Farm. The wall with its cock-and-hen coping was not particularly comfortable to sit on but there was one spot where the copings were spaced just right . That was the place I headed for. The traffic was such that we could collect almost every car number and the make of car. The vehicles tended to come in batches, held up by a slow one in front. Between batches we sat and waited until we heard another lot approaching in the distance. In between times we consulted our AA books to see where the cars came from. Most were registered in Dorset so carried the letters FX, JT, PR and JK on their number plate. For example JFX 106 (my first car) was a Dorset registered vehicle. It probably seems a pointless exercise but it passed the time and we enjoyed doing it.

All children collected postage stamps. The main aim was to collect as many as we could. Packets of stamps could be bought in Woolworths but as we got more expert we preferred to go to Mr Gale's stamp shop in South Street to buy specific stamps. George Hyde, Bryan's father, was a keen collector and member of the Bridport Stamp Club. He gave us good advice and let us look through the boxes of loose stamps that he received through the post. He would spread them on the table so that we could pick out a few that we fancied. They were not very expensive so our collections built up quickly. Approval books were popular, they came through the post. There was no obligation to buy but we were happy to spend our pocket money on a lot of colourful but generally worthless material.

The apple orchards were an attraction particularly when the apples were ripe. Unfortunately most were for cider making so were not good to eat. I think the enjoyment came from the risk of being caught, or not. On one occasion a few of us were caught red-handed by Mr Rice-Oxley, the farmer at Knowle Farm. He bellowed "Come here boys" which we meekly did as he knew us and our parents. We trotted over expecting a good telling off. We were surprised when, instead, he told us that the apples we were trying to knock off the tree were not ripe but there were plenty of fallers from other trees that were ready for eating and we could have some of those as we wanted. I'm not sure if we were relieved or disappointed but we took a couple each just to be polite.

We liked to "help on the farms". Uncle Frank, who lived next door, was a carter at Upton Manner Farm and as the horses were phased out he

drove the tractors including the Field Marshall with its very distinctive low revving engine noise; phut-phut-phut, and so on and on. At harvest time we went along to watch and "help". The reaper-binder started cutting from the outside of the field and worked its way towards the middle. It cut the corn and tied in to sheaves. We ran on behind stacking the sheaves in to stooks (left) ready to be collected and taken for threshing. This was another thing we enjoyed watching.

As the binder worked away the area of standing corn got smaller and smaller so that the rabbits hiding in the corn moved towards the middle. Eventually the frightened rabbits made a dash. One or two to begin with but as the corn almost disappeared they ran out in all directions zig-zagging as they went. Then the chase began. Farm workers, helpers and spectators gave chase armed with knob-ended sticks in an attempt to catch a rabbit or two for dinner. The success rate was usually fairly high.

Cousin Maureen Crabb lived next door and as neither of us had siblings we were almost like brother and sister. Aged about three (right) we are standing outside the wash-house at West View (Killick Cottage).

All children looked forward to birthdays and the chance of a good tea. Maureen and Helen Ward who lived next door to her and I had an odd sequence of birth dates. My birthday is 6 June, Helen's 7 July and Maureen's 8 August which are 6/6, 7/7 and 8/8. The years will remain undisclosed to protect the ladies. All I will say that Helen and I are just over a year older than Maureen.

(Below) Helen Ward's birthday party (10th ?) with her family and friends from the village and Bridport Convent School where she was a pupil. It's outside Johnwyn (now Christmas Cottage) where the Ward family lived.
(Back) Aunt Sally Read, Winnie Ward (née Read) with Isobel "Bunch" Ward, Aunt Dorothy Broom (née Read). In front of Bunch is Ruth Willmott.
(Middle) Pauline Dunkerton, Mary Willmott, Rosemary Hyde; Bryan Hyde, Bernard Paull. (Bryan and I were slightly outnumbered by the girls!)
(Front) Helen Ward, Rosamond Willmott, Lynette Driver, Moira Derryman, Maureen Crabb.

Sunday School

Sunday School for children up to the age of 11 was held in Loders Church on Sunday afternoons. Mrs Willmott, who was in charge, made it an enjoyable hour or so, when our parents had a bit of peace and quiet.

During the summer holidays we had the Sunday School outing arranged with military precision by Mrs Willmott. We almost always went to Weymouth. With its sandy beach, shallow water, buckets and spades, Punch and Judy, donkey ride, floats, candy floss and crowds of trippers just like us what more could we want. The beach became very crowded so it was easy to get lost. The solution was the 'Loders Sunday School' flag to mark our pitch. It was a good day out and the weather was always sunny. Well, that's how I remember it! (Below) The Loders Sunday School party in 1954.

Back rows from left: Mrs Osborne, -?-, Mrs Pavey (Mrs Osborne's daughter), Phyllis Bunnell, Mrs Willmott, Edna Driver, Christine Harris, Caroline Elliott, Ena Crabb, Ruth Willmott, -?-, Frank Good with flag, Mary Gill, Dora Hyde under flag, and right at the end Annie Paull, my mother

Along front the smaller children: Ingrid Burrell, Teresa Pavey, ? Pavey In the pushchair, Annelie Burrell, Lynette Driver, Janette Bolton, Chuck Willmott (with blonde curls), Mary Willmott, Helen Ward, Maureen Crabb, Kenny Drake (?), Rosamund Willmott, Annabel Howell, Evelyn Elliott, David Gill (?), Bryan Hyde, me between Bryan Hyde and Brian Bolton, Michael Willmott, Maurice Matterface, Juliet Willmott, -?- , -?-, Susan Elliott, Morwenna Willmott, Dianne Tiltman(?).

(Right) On the Sunday School outing, or maybe just day out, enjoying a ride on the donkeys on Weymouth beach.

(From the left) Bernard Paull, Maureen Crabb, Helen Ward and her little sister Isobel (Bunch) Ward.

In 1954 the cost of the Sunday School outing was met from a house-to-house collection around the village. Just over £15 was collected which covered the cost of the coach, a boat trip around Portland Harbour and tea on the beach for 30 children. After spending eight hours in Weymouth followed by a hot and sticky coach journey back to Loders we arrived home sunburnt, weary, a bit niggly and almost ready for bed. It had been a very good day.

Mothering Sunday was another of the big events. A couple of days before we went off to the fields and along the lanes to pick primroses from the hedgerows. We tied them in small bunches, wrote a label to our mother and attached it as neatly as we could to the bunch. On Mothering Sunday our mothers were invited to the morning service and presented with the flowers by their child. A very simple and personal procedure, no commercialisation, no money spent, no Mothering Sunday cards but our mums were invariably moist eyed as they were given their little bunch of flowers. They appreciated the effort that we had shown and our appreciation of them.

There were always bunches left over on Mothering Sunday. These were distributed to the elderly and those who were in poor health. I'm sure those on their own appreciated an unexpected visit as much as the primroses.

When we grew too old for Sunday School we joined the Church Choir. This involved junior choir practice on Thursday evenings and attending the Sunday morning service. Mr Tiltman, the organist, did his best to get us to sing in tune but, in my case, without too much success. On winter evenings it was dark at the start of choir practice. To begin with, we were slightly apprehensive and walked warily but quickly through the unlit graveyard towards the lights in the church. We soon realised there was nothing to fear but there was the opportunity of hiding behind the tombstones and trying to frighten other unsuspecting members of the choir. As we got older and wiser we grew out of such childish pursuits.

Bonfire Night

Guy Fawkes night was a reason for a good bonfire. The local farmers Messrs Crabb and Rice-Oxley were very obliging and allowed us to build huge bonfires on their land. Sometimes we were able to help ourselves to hedge cuttings that just happened to be nearby. This was an important factor on our choice of site! Bonfire night usually fell in the half-term week which gave us plenty of time to collect rubbish from home and around the village. The 1959 bonfire (above) built by Tommy Dennett, David Gill, Bryan Hyde, Bernard Paull, David Skeats and Ronald Tilley was memorable. It featured in the December 1959 Reverend Willmott's Parish Notes, extract below.

By universal consent the best bonfire was at Shatcombe. It had been assembled with an industry which, if only it could be applied to lessons, would surely land the boys in the university. Ronald Tilley capped it with a few gallons of used motor oil, and the resulting blaze was colossal. Here again, it seems that the older people (and of these there are not a few in Uploders) enjoyed it most. Said 83 year old Mrs Wallbridge: "When Ernest and I went to our beds that night, we didn't want the light on, t'were that bright we opened our windows and let the heat in, and really Mr Willmott, t'were the first time our old bones have really bin warm this winter". If the owners of Mrs Wallbridge's cottage should read this, and subsequently detect a lot of blistered paint, they would, we trust, not lay it to the charge of the boys, but write it off as an "Act of God.

Mrs Wallbridge and Ernest (Ern) Hawkins outside their house at Shatcombe. It was claimed that their parrot, Loretta, was 100 years old and could recite the Lord's Prayer. I cannot confirm this but I do know that Loretta had knowledge of some less savoury words. According to unconfirmed rumours, she once used a few of these to greet the vicar; and survived!

Earning a Few Coppers

Like most children I received weekly pocket money to spend on the things I could not do without; sweets comics, model planes and the like. Visiting uncles and aunts boosted my income when they slipped two-bob or half-crown in my hand as they left. Postal orders that arrived at Christmas or on my birthday were gratefully received. They were acknowledged with polite thank-you letters written, usually, after a number of "Have you written your thank-you letters yet ?".

Neighbours, Aunty Ena and Uncle Frank Crabb, let Ern Hawkins (pictured on page 36) use a part of their garden to grow vegetables. Ern was a bit rheumatic and could not move very quickly or bend too well so I sometimes gave him a hand on his plot. At the end of one season he was struggling with his pea-sticks so he asked for help to tie up his 'stickers' to take home for kindling. This I did and trotted along the road beside him in his 'girt' (great-big) hobnail boots carrying a bundle of stickers. For my troubles a twelve-sided brass 'thrup-penny' bit, came my way. I was very pleased!

It was usual practice for the older children to escort the younger ones to school something Pauline Legg, a very sensible and responsible girl, did for me. When I reached an age when I was deemed to be sensible and responsible I took on a similar role with Pauline's brother, Mervyn. Mrs Legg, his mother, kindly gave me the occasional sixpence for my troubles; my first regular paid income!

A lovely but very deaf old lady, Mrs D'Alcorn, lived in Sunnyside, the cottage next to the Yondover railway bridge (right). From the age of about 13 or 14 I helped her in the garden on Saturday mornings. I mowed the lawn, weeded, trimmed the river bank and with some supervision, pruned her rambling roses, trees and shrubs. She gave me half a crown, not bad money then, a glass of Robinson's Barley Water, a biscuit and sometimes a slice of cake. Many years later Marjorie Randall arrived on our doorstep with a package, a wedding present from Mrs D'Alcorn. It was a silver-plated cruet set, one of her own belongings. We still treasure it now. She was poorly at the time and sadly passed away soon afterwards. I still think of her when I drive past Sunnyside.

Before leaving school, I did various jobs during the school holidays and at weekends. I delivered mail at Christmas and carried out bar, kitchen and domestic work at the West Bay Hotel, the latter for half-a-crown an hour or ten-bob (50p) for a Sunday morning's work. Factory work in Beaminster was another job. We travelled from Bridport on the works bus. On one occasion it was delayed and so we clocked-in a few minutes late for which we were docked a quarter-of-an-hour's pay. We considered this to be totally unjust so spoke to the management pointing out that we had no control over lateness. The company bus was at fault. We were told very firmly "Late was late!". It was not much money to lose but to us the principle was totally unreasonable. We had to accept the decision, we had no option. The outcome was disgruntled workers with, I'm sure, an associated drop in productively. Hopefully we all learnt a lesson from what was a trivial event; I believe I did. Having said that I enjoyed working there, everyone was friendly and during the summer we played cricket on the school playing field at lunch-time, which was fun.

Loders Court

From a young age Loders Court featured in the lives of the villagers. Around about Christmas time Sir Edward and Lady Le Breton invited the children of the village to the 'Court Party'. A coach picked up those from outlying areas which included Uploders. On arrival at the Court we were escorted in to the Billiard Room. Sir Edward welcomed us and introduced the entertainment. A Punch and Judy Show (alright for the little kids was our thought as we got older) was followed by a conjuror who pulled rabbits out of hats and other magic tricks. It must have been magic, what else could it have been? Then followed the tea; sandwiches, iced buns and meringues with cream. They really were the icing on the cake!

Sometime during the afternoon one unfortunate was approached, by the Reverend Willmott and asked to give the vote of thanks. Although we really appreciated the party it was a time most of us, rather ungratefully, wished we were invisible, mainly because we lived in fear of drying-up part way through our speech. Eventually my turn came to be asked. I spent most of the tea-time mentally putting something together and, as a result, suffered from a partial loss of appetite.

Eventually the time came. I climbed to my feet and started off "On behalf of........etc, etc" and ended up with what the others had said in previous years "Three cheers to Sir Edward and Lady Le Breton, hip-hip" and the others went "Hooray", three times. Amazingly it went without a major hitch (you will be disappointed to hear) and I had survived. As usual the party was reported in Mr Willmott's Parish Notes which I read with some trepidation only to discover that I had been given a very favourable review! It read:- *".....The vote of thanks was made by Bernard Paull, who shewed promise of making a good after dinner speaker".* Not unexpectedly my 'friends' were quick to give me their appraisals!

On leaving the Court Party we were all presented with an orange, an apple and half-crown, 12.5 pence in new money. A half crown was enough for one of the better, but not the best, seats at the Palace or Lyric cinemas, an ice-cream at the interval and still have a few coppers left over.

Loders Fête was, and still is, held on the first Saturday of August at Loders Court. The fête has almost always been blessed with dry weather. The Reverend Willmott hoped, and possibly prayed, for a dry but overcast day so that folks did not head for the beach in preference to the fête. When we were old enough we helped with the children's games and the like. In the 1940s and early 50s gymkhanas were held in the Park. It was much the same as it is today but without the cars or the pop-up beer tent.

When we reached our early teens the boys of Loders and Bradpole were allowed to use the billiard table, the tennis court and, when we were about 15, the squash court.

The door to the Billiard Room was off the veranda (see below). It was a large room that smelt of cigar smoke with the billiard table at one end. The other end was fairly clear of furniture, just a few armchairs and a settee. A few pairs of boxing gloves were scattered on a side table for anyone who fancied a fight. Most of us tried it once or twice but decided we preferred snooker and billiards rather than a punch on the nose!
We spent many summer evenings playing tennis, sometimes until it was almost dark. Some evenings the tennis court was reserved for other groups, the staff from the Bridport Railway Station was one, but if they didn't turn up we were free to move in.

The squash court was one of very few in the area. Several school friends cycled out to Loders on Saturday afternoons for a game. Peter Gregory and Richard (Rick) Wills (later my best man) joined the village boys Brian Bolton and me. We were not particularly sophisticated to begin with and Peter ended up with smashed glasses from an over enthusiastic back-swing; something you should not do in squash. When we had improved we had games against Sir Edward. He was in his mid-seventies and not particularly mobile. We were about 16 and fairly fit but we had no answer to his skill. He dominated the centre of the court so that we were forced to run round him to every corner of the court. Red faced and dripping sweat we were hammered but we learnt a few tricks to add to our skills. It was not many years later in 1961 that Sir Edward sadly passed away.

1953 - The Coronation and Television

One of the most memorable events in the 1950s was the Queen's Coronation on Tuesday 2 June 1953.

Very few people had television sets but those who did kindly invited those who didn't to their houses to watch this historic event. About 40 of us joined the Rice-Oxley's at Knowle Farm to watch the black and white pictures on a 12 or 14 inch screen in its sturdy wooden cabinet.

There was local interest in the ceremony. Colonel Sir Edward Le Breton from Loders Court was a Gentleman-at-Arms at the Coronation, they lined the route in the Chancel of Westminster Abbey. He brought back the blue screens which were placed behind the alter in Loders Church.

Houses in the village were decorated with red, white and blue flags, bunting and pictures of the Queen. At 3.30pm on the afternoon of Coronation Day a colourful fancy dress parade set off from Matravers bound for Loders Court.

(Above) The parade led by Frank Good marches past the Chapel and Knowle Farm in Uploders. Over his left shoulder is Dora Legg, behind and in-line with the telegraph pole is Phyllis Bunnell (née Thomas). The man in the suit and trilby hat on the left is Alby (Tubby) Wells with Edna Driver (née Baker) alongside him.

At Loders Court tea, cakes and soft drinks were provided. Sports and games included a tug-of-war across the river.

Every child in the village was presented with a Coronation mug, a gift from Sir Edward and Lady Le Breton.

The mugs were inscribed on the back 'From Col. Sir Edward and Lady Le Breton'. In the absence of Sir Edward they were handed over by his grandson, Edward Laskey.

In the evening entertainment and much merriment took place in the Hut which was decorated with red, white and blue flags and bunting. Fireworks and a bonfire on Mr Crabb's field across the road ended the celebrations.

Luckily most of the few who purchased or rented televisions did so at least a few weeks before the Coronation which meant that on 2 May 1953 mainly the men of the village and their sons (there was very little political correctness in those days) were invited to watch the Cup Final. Blackpool beat Bolton Wanderers 4-3 to great national acclaim as Stanley Mathews had at last won a cup-winner's medal having been on the losing side twice before in the 1948 and 1951 finals.

The Mothers Union

A Christmas meeting c1952 in The Ex-Servicemen's Hut. Centre at the table is Mrs Wells. Standing from the left -?-, Mrs Crabb, Olive Legg, -?-, Phyllis Bunnell, Mrs Willmott, Enid Crabb, -?-, Pearl Symes. Sitting from the left 4th Netta Taylor, 8th Marjorie Gale, 11th Mabel Skeats, 14th May Osborne, 16th Lizzie Crabb.

The Loders Arms Skittles Team

Cup winners c1955. (Back row from left) Fred Kick, Vernon Kick, Clem Poole, Bill Paull, (my father) Harold Darby, Sam Legg, Frank Osborne (Landlord). (Front row, sitting, from the left) Cecil Rogers and Dick Darby. There was no skittle alley at the Loders Arms then so the team must have played on away alleys.

The Women's Institute

In 1960 the Loders WI celebrated its 13th birthday. The picture below was taken at Loders Mill in 1947, the year that the Loders WI was re-established.

Those present are (from the left: back row) Miss Holmes, -?-, Lady Le Breton, Mrs Ebbs, May Osborne, Netta Taylor, Amy Darby, Joan Scott, Mrs Bond, Sis Gale, Ann Crabb, Lizzie Crabb, Mrs Pitcher, Mrs Wells, Mrs Swaffield, Mrs Townsend, Mrs Crabb and Miss Butterworth.
(Front) Miss Hinks, -?-, Olive Legg, Mrs Holmes, Mrs Whittle, Mrs Tiltman, Mrs Moon, Nellie Crabb, Mrs Willmott, Grannie Hyde, Grace Hyde, Dora Hyde, Mrs Dick Hyde, Mrs Thomas, Mrs Payvey, -?-, Mrs Pitcher, Elsie Poole, Edith Hinks.
(Standing), Mrs Dimend and Grannie Crabb. The children are Rosemond and Mary Willmott, Bryan Hyde and Jannette Bond.

Loders Women's Institute at Loders Court in about 1950 as guests of Lady Le Breton. (Seated in the front row from the left) Kate Bourne, Miss Shaw and Lady Le Breton. (Second row standing) -?-, Pearl Symes, Jean Budden, Mrs Lenthall, Sylvia Hyde, Granny Crabb, Adele Hyde, Cis Gale and Mrs Lesser.
(Behind the second row) Netta Taylor, Olive Legg, Gladys Budden, Edith Hinks, Marjorie Randall(?), -?-. -?-, Lady Le Breton's sister.

Askerswell & District Young Farmers Club (AYFC)

Contributed by Elizabeth Gale, neé Buckler

The Askerswell and District Young Farmers' Club was founded on 4th December 1936 by George Jesse a farmer from Askerswell, already familiar with the movement in Sussex, Colonel Wordsworth, the Reverend Pope, a dozen other local prominent farmers and Ralph Wightman, the Dorset broadcaster, author and commentator, friend of the Lenthalls of Upton Manor Farm. The Club was run at first by an adult advisory committee with a junior chairman, the first being Bill Dawe, who farmed at North Eggardon. The Askerswell schoolroom was hired at four shillings per evening for meetings where some twenty members were welcomed.

The original aims were to educate the young farmers, most from typical West Dorset family farms, in cattle husbandry and calf rearing. Lloyds Bank advanced the money to purchase twenty-six Shorthorn calves at Sturminster Market averaging £3 to £5 each and members drew lots to secure one to rear and show. At the first calf show, held at Dorchester Market, the best heifer prize was awarded to Walter Bishop of Yondover, Loders.

During the Second World War some meetings were postponed as members were busy on the land. Outings were curtailed but money for the Red Cross Society was raised by holding a dance, at Askers Road House, tickets 3/6d. During the war, members collected waste paper and farm safety talks featured. To reduce the number of windows to black-out, the venue was moved to Loders Parish Room adjacent to the Crown Inn in Uploders. West of England sacks made ideal black-out material! Land Girls were invited to meetings and a number stayed on after the war.

The Club membership had grown by 1945 and the calf showing was allowed to fade out as other competitions were taking prominence. A larger hall was needed and the move to the more central Loders Hut was made. Quite chilly with a knotted floor, precarious stage, simple kitchen cum dressing room facilities, an Elsan lavatory and a single tap; it was of its day, perfectly suitable, an asset to the village and many happy times were spent there. Well-known speakers and demonstrators came along and there were visits to go-ahead farms. Modern agricultural methods were advised.

An inter-club Rally took place in the Marshwood Vale with competitions for boys in field contests and in a tent where the girls competed in home crafts. The day ended with County President Rolf Gardiner, a flax growing expert and his wife vigorously leading Morris Dancing.

Rolf Gardiner had a great affection for the Askerswell Club and initiated a Harvest Supper in Loders Hut for guests, members and parents. The room was decorated with hedgerow foliage and in spite of being a wooden building it was brilliantly lit by candles. The parents provided the food which consisted of cold roast chicken, game birds, venison, home-killed pork, trifles, home-made bread, cheese and butter, cider and home-made wine. Muriel Randall led the proceedings and produced an entertainment. At the end of the evening members undertook the washing-up in tin bowls in the very basic kitchen.

The Harvest Supper then became a highly contested Inter-Club County Federation competition for the coveted Rolf Gardiner Loving Cup with other challenges springing up to fill the programme such as public speaking, entertainment, hedging, milking, stock-judging, the annual inter-club rally and overall the huge Upton Oil Cup for the most proficient club. Over the years Askerswell took these various trophies time and time again. At one stage the Upton Cup came home to Loders three times in close succession. Edgar Bishop was one of several popular Club Leaders.

In 1951, local Boarsbarrow farmer's son, Clifford Pitcher was elected Chairman and remained in office for three years during the Club's heyday. He owned a car and it could often be seen loaded with the young folk; bicycles being the usual means of transport. Supporting him was a superb team of members who participated in everything.

Through the 1950s the Club dominated the County movement. The girls made and embroidered Hessian sack skirts to wear at a harvest supper. Several members journeyed on exchange visits to other countries. Visits were made by Dutch girls and the Exeter Young Farmers' Club when Albert (Tubby) Wells, was president of the Askerswell club.

(Above) The 1953 Harvest Supper in Loders Hut with (left to right): - Chairman Clifford Pitcher, President Martin Lenthall, Club Leader Alan Musgrove and Secretary Elizabeth Buckler (Gale).

(Above) The Follies entertainment at the Harvest Supper in 1953 which went on to win the County competition. Left to right the cast are, Jessie Crabb (Barrett), Doreen Barnes (Doble), Bill Hounsell (standing), Elizabeth Buckler (Gale), Bill Ives, Clifford Pitcher and Beryl Curran (Samways).

Visit of the Exeter Young Farmers Club in 1957. (Front, from the left) Tubby Wells, Monica Page and Daphne Cooper. Immediately behind are Chairman Elizabeth Buckler (Gale), Exeter YFC Chairman, Guy Gale, AYFC Vice-Chairman, Ann Groves, Jennifer Aldridge. Standing at the back are, Mavis Woodward, Audrey Marsh, Margaret Barnes, David Curran and Miriam Bugler.

Farmers lent land on which potatoes were grown, harvested and sold to raise funds; it was a time of high activity. Over the years there were several marriages within the Club.

In 1957 the Club's 21st birthday was celebrated at Askers Road House, on a wet, cold and foggy December evening. The celebrations took the form of a dinner, "This is Your Life" entertainment featuring the Club, dancing and cutting a decorated cake, resembling a farmyard. Marjorie Randall then working in Africa sent a surprise congratulatory cable.

When the membership reached eighty in the late 1950s, Loders Hut was almost outgrown. For the larger events the club moved to Burton Bradstock W.I. Hall and meetings were held at the Conservative Rooms in Bridport.

However, Loders Hut was often put to good use, such as in 1962 there was a great evening when the visiting Dutch Agricultural students were given a party there. The Hut, hung with lines of newspaper, was ideal for a tramp-theme fish and chips supper, too. (Above) The Dutch Students washing outside the Hut before the party.

Still the success and education continued into the 1960s but the older troupe had moved on having reached twenty-six, the upper age limit for membership. By 1965/66 the numbers had dwindled and it was decided that there were far more youngsters in the Bride Valley and a new organisation was started there.

Askerswell and District Young Farmers' Club's notable existence was brought to a close after thirty years, with a Thanksgiving Service in Loders Church, conducted by the Reverend Oliver Willmott. That final evening concluded with a bittersweet party in Loders Hut, a display of old photographs and a toast to the future

My Boyhood memories of David Skeats.

In August 2018 one of my childhood friends, David Skeats, sadly passed away in Norfolk where he had lived for many years. As his family in Norfolk knew very little about his childhood I was asked by Alan Symes to write a few words about his life when he was a boy. This I did and it was read out at his funeral and I received a letter of thanks from one of his daughters. I have decided to include this tribute to David in his memory and as a reminder of what life was like for small boys in the 1950s.

(Left) David's mother Mabel Symes (Skeats) and my mother (right) Annie Hawker (Paull) in about 1925 were friends who grew up together in Uploders and went to the village school in Loders. They both married during the war and David and I came along close together so it was no surprise that we too became good friends.

(Right) From the left, my mother with me and Mabel Skeats with David at West Bay in about 1947

David grew up at 3 Box Cottages in the small West Dorset village of Loders. His Aunty Bertha lived at 1 Box Cottages and other aunts, uncles and cousins lived nearby. This was how it had been for generations.

At the age of five he went to the nearby Loders School where maths was one of his best subjects. It was a small school with only 25 to 30 pupils aged between 5 and 11 and, for much of the time, with just one teacher.

During a hot spell in the summer holidays when we were about eight we decided that as we could not go to the sea-side we would make our own pond. The original idea was a swimming pool but we quickly realised that this was being slightly over ambitious! David's father, Derek, was in the process of rearranging the back garden so everything was at hand to dig a large hole which we banked up with soil dug from the hole. At the back of 2 Box Cottages was the communal pump used by the three cottages. There was no mains water in the village then so we got busy pumping water into buckets in an endeavour to fill the pond. Being unlined the water disappeared as soon as it was tipped in. Undeterred we carried on until the whole area was a sticky, muddy mess and we were covered in mud from head to toe. David's mother, Mabel, appeared and we were both given a good telling off and I was sent home only to receive another even sterner one!

Outside school we had no formal parks or playground. Everywhere within reach was our playground. Like all young boys David enjoyed exploring the lanes and fields around the village always accompanied by his faithful black dog 'Nipper' a friendly animal of very mixed breeding. The river Asker, which ran along the bottom of our gardens, was also a source of fun; fishing, generally messing around and getting wet and muddy. All the things that children enjoy.

David was a very keen cyclist which gave him the means to explore further afield to Bridport, West Bay and beyond. Burton Bradstock with its shingle beach and the sea was a favourite. The journeys were often planned to visit one of his many aunts and uncles who would welcome him with a drink and a biscuit.

In our early teens we joined the Youth Hostel Association (YHA) and set off on our bikes to spend a few days in the Mendips; Cheddar, Wookey Hole, Wells etc. There was no means of keeping in touch with home as neither of our parents had telephones. Very few did then. Looking back, it was not surprising that our parents seemed very relieved when we arrived home safely!

During the summer holidays, David often went to London to stay with his aunt Amy and her family. They ran a newsagents and David enjoyed helping on the paper delivery rounds. His two cousins, Marilyn and Colin

Metcalfe occasionally stayed with Aunt Bertha at 1 Box Cottages. Colin being a year or two older than us and coming from London was much more street-wise than we boys from the country and so we followed his leadership to become much more adventurous. As well as our usual summer pursuits, cricket, walks with the dog and generally doing very little. I remember our attempts to build a dam across the River Asker. We were not successful, which is probably just as well, but it kept us occupied, wet and happy for several days.

Like most children in those days David was a keen stamp collector and was a junior member of the Bridport Stamp Club. He was a tough negotiator in stamp swapping. It was never a straight one for one exchange but was based on the valuation of the stamps from the Stanley Gibbons' catalogue. This often resulted in a much-heated debate!

David also enjoyed card games, Rummy and Newmarket come to mind and in wet and cold weather long afternoons were spent at the Monopoly board. The competition was always very keen and we were all bad losers!

On leaving Loders School he moved on to the newly opened Alfred Colfox School, a comprehensive and one of the first in the county. As well as his school work he found the time for a job delivering the Dorset Evening Echo around the village. At the Colfox School he spent five years in the top class for his year before taking his O-levels and moving to work in London.

It was the parting of the way for us but I still recall our boyhood years with much fondness.

Bernard Paull

26th August 2018

PART II
The Earlier Years
Life in Loders c1900 to c1950

Loders is a picturesque village lying in the Asker Valley about 3 miles from Bridport. This rural community grew up along the road that follows the River Asker and served the numerous farms in the area. The village is made up of three areas, Uploders in the east, Lower Loders in the west and Yondover in the middle.

An aerial view of the Asker Valley from Upton Farm to Lower Loders.

Uploders

In the early 1900s Uploders boasted the Chapel, the Parish (School) Room, a blacksmith, two carriers, two public houses and a shop.

Postcard by the Bridport photographer Claude Hider c1930 of the eastern end of Uploders looking southwards across the River Asker. The barn that was converted to a house in 2019 is on the right of the picture.

The Cattistock Hunt c1950 led by Edgar Bishop of Yondover Farm on the road between Uploders and Askerswell just west of Folly Cottage.

Matravers

Aerial photograph with Matravers Farm buildings and Matravers Farmhouse. Matravers Bungalow overlooks the road junction. The road to the left led to Sheepwash where the sheep were dipped before being sheared.

Matravers bungalow built in the 1940s for Mr and Mrs Herbert Bartlett on their retirement from Croads Farm. Mr Bartlett was a cattle dealer as well as a farmer.

Matravers House in 1936 with Mr and Mrs Lesser strolling in their garden with visitors.

Upton Manor Farm

The Dairy House fire in 1935. The ridge pole to the left of the chimney remains unburnt. Fires were a not infrequent occurrence in the village. Many resulted from sparks on to thatch from house chimneys or passing steam engines. The fires always created a lot of local interest!

Picture taken c1950 showing the Dairy House in the right-hand middle distance. Jack Crabb was the Dairyman. He replaced Percival (Percy) Bowditch in 1946.

Upton Manor Farmhouse

Aerial photograph of Upton Manor farmhouse and farm buildings. The houses in the foreground are Upton Peep and Water Cleaves.

Upton Manor Farmhouse looking from the south. The picture was taken between 1907 and 1918 when Mr Edwin Randall was the Farmer. The farm employed a number of farmworkers. Most lived nearby in tied farm cottages.

The North Devon Reds

Colin Bowditch the son of Percival (Percy) Bowditch, Head Dairyman at Upton from 1941 to 1946, gave this information on the Devon Reds. This breed made up the herd during Percy Bowditch's time at Upton.

This picture was taken up to 50 years before the one below. The person holding the bull is likely to be the farmer or farm manager. The head stockman is standing a little away ready to grab the horns or halter if the bull began some antics. He is wearing boots and gaiters rather than a top hat and long coat. The animals look very different, the one above is of a really ancient type of beast, narrow shoulders and horns that would not be tolerated in a conventional herd. The bull below is definitely of the improved Devon Red Ruby breed. The breeding has concentrated the horn shape so that it is less obtrusive in a herd context. It's also a better shape for both milk production and with some beef characteristics.

Working at Upton Manor Farm

Farmer, Edwin Edward Randall at Upton Manor Farm with his farm workers c1912. The farmer's name is on the wagon on the left. The other contains apples for cider making. The men (left to right) are George Randall, Arthur Hansford, Alf Crabb, Jim Hawker, Eddie Hansford, George Hawker and Edwin Randall. These were just a few of the farm workers at that time.

Farm workers, c1920, with long handled ditching spades. Ditches around the fields were dug out and the soil used to build up the adjacent hedge banks. Second from the right is Elias (Alec) Peach, born in 1885.

The ford on the Asker at Upton Farm with Jim Hawker (right) and Alf Crabb and the working horses. The picture dates from between 1910 and 1918 when Edwin Randall was the Farmer. In 2018 the ford was replaced with a bridge when the road was realigned away from a landslip area.

Sheep-shearing at Chilcombe c1900. Although not in Loders similar scenes would have been seen at Upton Manor Farm as the farm kept sheep and had its own shepherd. The shearers, (above) could have done the same job in Loders.

The advert below appeared in numerous newspapers, including the Hereford Journal, in January 1900. Working on the farm took its toll and clearly, James (Jim) Hawker (left) my mother's uncle, had found an instant cure to all his problems and, no doubt, suitable recompense from the makers of Dr Williams' Pink Pills! His wife Annie who is quoted is pictured above, on the right.

The Pains of a Life of Agriculture.

RHEUMATISM, A COMMON COMPLAINT AMONG WORKERS ON THE LAND, IS CURED BY DR. WILLIAMS' PINK PILLS.

A RECENT article in the "Bridport News" contained the characteristic history of a Dorsetshire worthy, James Hawker, of Upper Loders, near Bridport. "I want everybody to know," he said—and it was an interesting story that the reporter listened to.

"I used to be terrible bad," said Mr. Hawker, "what with rheumatism and bleeding at the nose—oh! for eighteen months or more, and not a week without it. But I've not had it now since last March."

"Ah!" said Mrs. Hawker from the corner, "Jim's another man now. He used to have rheumatism so bad he couldn't lift his arms to dress himself. But I saw something in a little book about rheumatism being cured by Dr. Williams' Pink Pills, and, as poor Jim couldn't get anything to ease him, I thought he should try the pills, as it said they were good for that. He'd tried nearly everything, and had been doctoring for years."

"Ay, that's right enough," said Mr. Hawker; "and when she showed me a box of 'em, and said they would do me good, I laughed. They looked such little bits of things. But I took them, though I looked on it more as a joke than anything, and said to the missus I'd take the box and all."

"Ah! Jim laughed at me; but it turned out right. I used to have a job with him, and got anything I could, including embrocation; but nothing did him any good, and I began to feel he never would be right. It was a blessing I saw that little book about Dr. Williams' Pink Pills."

"That's right enough," added Mr. Hawker, "and you can't think how I feel about those pills. I was easier after the first lot. I said, 'By Jove, missus! I believe they're the thing for me now, for I seem looser about the shoulders already.' That was a day or two after I began taking them. And so I went on, and—would you believe it?—when I had taken two boxes and a half I was as right and as well as ever I was. I'd been suffering for years, and some mornings I couldn't lift my arms up to my head. I hardly knew myself when I got rid of the pain. The change the pills brought about was wonderful, and I tell everybody about it, because I think if folks knew more about them it

would be better for them, and save a lot of pain and expense."

Mrs. Hawker concluded that her husband couldn't stoop to chop a stick without his nose bleeding. "And you know, sir," she added, "I got frightened about it, because I've heard it brings on fits. Besides, it kept him so weak. If I have anything wrong with me I take some of Dr. Williams' Pink Pills, and they soon pull me together again."

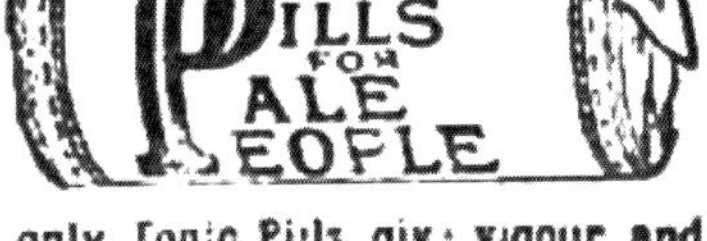

the only Tonic Pills, give vigour and increased working capacity both to Men and Women. Price 2s. 9d. per box, or six boxes for 13s. 9d. To avoid substitutes, look for the full name (seven words). If desired, Dr. Williams' Pink Pills for Pale People may be ordered direct from the Dr. Williams' Medicine Company, Holborn Viaduct, London. These pills have cured, up to the end of December 1899,

West of Upton Manor Farm

The construction of the new house in the meadow alongside the River Asker just west of Upton Manor Farmhouse. This replaced the two old cottages that previously stood on the site. The 1890 Ordnance Survey map shows stepping stones across the river. These were later replaced with a wooden footbridge. The cottages were the homes of farmworkers at Upton Farm including my grandfather, George Hawker and his brother Jim.

(Left) Dorothy Read (Broom), a great friend of my mother, sitting on the railings that separated the road from the steep bank that fell away to the river. Just beyond where Dorothy is sitting is the gap in the railings where the footpath ran down to the footbridge for Field Cottages.

Dorothy had three sisters, Winnie, Sally and Margaret and a brother, Percy. They lived in the cottage at the bottom of Lock's Lane, now called Briar Cottage.

Uploders House

Uploders House was built in the early 1700s by the Travers family on the site of an earlier house. It was extended in about 1820 with the addition of the Regency wing, pictured below. In the 1920s the staff included a butler, a footman, ladies' maids, grooms for the five horses, three gardeners and casual labour.

In 1959 the property was divided in two. The stables, coach-house and grooms' quarters became Bridgeacre, the remainder Uploders House. The latter was later divided when the original building (above left) retained the name Uploders House. The Regency wing, below viewed from the east, became Uploders Place.

1945 Welcome Home after the War

Children in fancy dress at Uploders House celebrating the end of the Second World War. John Lee carries a plaque that reads *"Just demobbed. WHAT IS IT TO BE THIS TIME WORK OR UNEMPLOYMENT?."* This relates to the fate of many servicemen who returned from the Great War in 1918.
From the left - Gwen Townsend, Tony Wells, Pam Crabb, Eileen Tilley, Maurice Crabb, Sheila Drake, Cathy Townsend, John Drake, Margaret Barnes, Margaret Steel, Beryl Tilley, John Lee, Janet Symes and Bernard Harris.

The younger children (back row) Margaret Hostler, Robin Wells, David Crabb, Janet Barnes, -?-. (Front row) Tony Yarde, Christine Harris, Jennifer White and Ann Hostler to the right of the dolls house. Maurice Crabb is standing in the background on the left, almost out of sight.

Near the Blacksmith's

Leonard and Mabel Collier alongside numbers 43, 44 and 45 Uploders. The village blacksmith occupied the single-storey building this side of the end house. On the right. The thatch on the cottages to the left was replaced with slate sometime later, see the picture below.

Banners across the road, flags on the house and in the garden in readiness for the Jubilee procession in 1935. Hillview has been enlarged and has a slate roof. The wooden building on the left is the workshop of Mr Ellis, the carrier.

Mr Ellis the Carrier

George Ellis outside his wooden bungalow, Cosy-Cot, located almost opposite the Forge in Uploders. Here he is with his faithful dog beside him at the end of a busy day fetching and carrying for the people in the village. Anyone needing his services would place a large "E" in their window for him to see as he passed by.

Times were changing! Mrs Mary Ellis standing proudly beside the smart van which had replaced her husband's horse and cart.

The Blacksmith

The last village blacksmith was Charlie Gale who worked from the Forge in Uploders. The picture (left) was taken before 1936 when Charlie worked for the then blacksmith, Bill Knight. It shows (from the left) Charlie Gale and Bill Knight, the boss, watching Bert Sheppick shoe a docile looking horse. A.E. Corbin, as on the cart, was the baker from Bradpole who delivered bread to nearby villages. Corbin's later became Caddy's. On the left is the old bonding platform used to put metal bands on wooden wagon wheels.

(Right) Blanche Knight, Bill Knight, looking slightly more portly than in the picture above, Charlie Gale, Bert Sheppick and Arthur Baggs outside the forge in about 1930.

(Right) Pearl Gale (Symes), Charlie's daughter on a grey. An array of new farm tools and implements are propped against the wall; rakes, pitch forks and a three legged milking stool. The local farmers relied on Mr Gale for new tools as well as repairs to their machinery and farm fittings. This was the age of repair and mend. There are still examples of Charlie Gale's work around the village including the gate at the Cemetery which was hung in 1937. These are a tribute to his skill and craftsmanship.

The Crown and Around

The Crown and surrounding area in about 1950. A lorry and car are parked in front of the Crown. The two large barns in Croads Farm (centre) look new. The Farmer here was Mr Herbert Bartlett. The garden opposite Croads Farm is now part of Purbeck Close. The large building next to Brook Barton in the 1940s and 50s was the workshop and dêpot of Mr Brown. He carried out road repairs and similar work. He also re-charged the accumulator batteries that were used to power the wireless. Prior to that it was the home and base of Steven Crabb, the carrier. In the 1930s and 40s he ran a local bus service.

(Right) Uploders Parish Room in the snow during the winter of 1962-63. It was located in New Road next to the Crown and was originally thatched.

The 1861 Census records it as a 'School House', a name still used by many folk in the 1950s. Before Loders School was built in 1869 it was the school for the Uploders children. Later it was a meeting room for the WI, Scouts, Discussion Group, the Askerswell Young Farmers, concerts, and auctioneers Morey's held auctions there. It was sold in 1972 for £3,750. The money was used to improve the Village Hall at Yondover. A house now stands on the site.

During the Second World War, Philip Symes and Roy Taylor collected scrap for the war-effort on their go-cart. Rags, bones, cans and metal were stored in the School House to be collected by the Council.

The Crown Inn

Up to the 1960s there were three other inns in the village; The Travellers Rest on the A35 and the Loders Arms and Farmers Arms in Lower Loders. Earlier there were at least three more establishments that served intoxicating liquor. Two inns, the Bell Inn and the Blue Ball on the A35 at the bottom of Stoney Head and a beer-house at Vinney Cross. In those days the landlord often had another job during the day leaving his wife to look after the bar when he was away. They were for the men; to drink, talk, play pub games and relax after work.

Postcard by Claude Hider showing the Crown in the late 1920s. The sign, below, reads 'Adelaide L Bartlett Licensed to Retail Beer, Ale, Cider, Spirituous Liquors & Tobacco'. The licence was later taken over by her son-in-law, Mr Tom Bourne. Inside the door a passageway led to the two small bars and a hatch, 'the jug and bottle' to serve liquor to take home.

Pine Cottages (now Springside Cottages)

Once three cottages, the two nearest the Crown, now Springside Cottage, had front doors side by side facing the road. The third, not in the pictures, is now Tiddly Cottage.

(Left) The most easterly cottage..

Water for nearby houses came from the chute, a pipe in the wall, just west of Tiddly Cottage.

(Below) The middle cottage with my great-grand-mother Ann Marsh (née Hansford) with John Hansford, her father and my great-great-grandfather. John was born in 1823 and died in 1901 so this picture must date from 1901 or earlier.

Ann Marsh died in 1949 and a nice and rather touching piece about her appeared in the May 1949 edition of the Reverend Willmott's Parish Notes:-

Mrs Ann Marsh, of the Bungalow, Uploders, was laid to rest on April 7th. She had reached the ripe age of 87. For twelve years she had been bedridden, crippled and blind. Yet she was one of the most cheerful of people in the village, rejoicing in the blessings of a good home, and always showing more interest in the lives of others than her own. A sweet and aristocratic soul—one who, like her Lord, was made perfect through suffering.

Riverdale and Westwards

In 1918 looking from Riverdale towards Box Cottages, a banner and flags mark the end of the First World War. Granny Hyde with one of her grandchildren, possibly George. Granny Hyde ran the village shop from this house well into the 1950s. It was demolished and replaced with the new house set back in the old orchard by George Hyde, her grandson. The two derelict cottages were destroyed by fire in April 1915. The cottages were occupied by Richard Gale and Wesley Hine and families.

(Right) The view from Box Cottages towards Riverdale in about 1922. Granny Hyde's house and shop with Polly's Cottage now Knight's Pightle just beyond.

The building adjoining Riverdale was once a black-smith's. Mr Knight was the last one.

Rose Cottage and The Trossachs (Butterwell)

Rose Cottage c1930s with a new thatched roof. The two 'X's on the wall are the ends of tie bars that were inserted through the house between the ground floor ceiling and the bedroom floor to support the walls. The bars were heated and the nuts on the threaded ends continually tightened. As the bars cooled they contracted and pulled the outer walls together. A job for the blacksmith.

The Trossachs (Butterwell) became the home of Farmer, Edwin Randall, and his wife when he retired from Upton Farm in 1918 until he died in 1931. Later Douglas V Duff lived here. He served in the Merchant Navy during World War I and survived being torpedoed on two occasions. He later rescued White Russian refugees from the Black Sea, spent time as an apprentice monk, served as a 'Black and Tan' in Ireland, and joined the Palestine Police. After further naval service in World War II, he became a successful broadcaster and author.

East from the Chapel

One of the Symes family, possibly Mabel, on the doorstep of 1 Box Cottages in about 1922 when the roof was still thatched. There were three cottages in the row, typical of that time, with two bedrooms in each. Water was pumped from a shared well at the back of the middle cottage. The fire damaged cottages near the bottom of the hill remain unrepaired. Picture by Potts.

A similar but later picture by Claud Hider. The fire damaged houses have been rebuilt but the roof of Box Cottages is still thatched so it's pre-1935. Another member of the Symes family, Phillip, stands on the doorstep of 1 Box Cottages.

Box Cottages

The middle cottage, c1930, has two bricked-up windows, presumably to reduce Window Tax. Other houses in the village had similar. They were often painted to appear like real windows; white frames and black panes. The middle cottage was the home of Walter Tudball, the village cobbler. His sign is over the door.

The thatch was removed in 1935 and replaced with slates. The original roof timbers were simple lengths of ash poles, a common feature at that time. The replacement roof would have been expensive but it eliminated the need to re- thatch, something that would be required every 30 or 40 years.

Easter Monday, 1939, Walter Tudball working on his garden with Mrs Emily Symes with her youngest son Rodney, his neighbours from next door. In the middle distance looking like two sentry boxes are the lavatories, earth-closets, for 1 and 2 Box Cottages. They were built in 1935 when the thatch was replaced.

To the right of Mrs Symes is Garden Cottage, the house by the river, It was the home of Frank and Rose Lush at about this time.

Happy Knowle Cottage and Bungalow

The 1901 edition of the Ordnance Survey map shows a cottage alongside Chapel Lane. Here the old thatched cottage is partially demolished, or was it damaged by fire? Oscar Gale with relative Rosa Jacobs and one of Harry Crabb's sons, either Ernest or Wilfred.

In 1938 Happy Knowle Bungalow next to the Chapel under construction by local builders, Montague's at a cost of £360. The bungalow replaced the cottage in the picture above. Sitting on the bay window is Bill Symes who once lived across the road in Box Cottages. Bert Swaffield is to his right.

Knowle Farm, Uploders

Knowle Farm in the 1930s. The photograph was taken from the Chapel looking westwards towards Myrtle Cottage. In the distance the pony and cart are probably those of one of the village carriers, most likely Mr Ellis or Steven Crabb who were both based in Uploders.

Mr Yarde, who managed the farm for Mr Bishop from Burton Bradstock, sitting on a milk-churn on the road outside Knowle Farm.

Officially the days of deliveries of milk from the farms were over. The milk was put into churns and collected by the local dairy, in this case the Devon and Somerset Dairies Ltd. The milk was treated by the dairy, bottled, sold in shops or delivered to the doorstep.

The 31 July 1978 was the last day on which the Milk Marketing Board collected milk churns. From then on all milk was collected by bulk transporters.

West of the Chapel

A mother and family at the door of what is now Christmas Cottage with other children posing on the dirt road c1905. The three cottages on the left each had two bedrooms, no bathroom, an outside lavatory and water from a shared well. Two of the old cottages have since combined to create Christmas Cottage. On the right the old cottage damaged by fire appears almost complete but covered in posters. Notice the cobbles in front of the cottages. The Wesleyan Methodist Chapel, built in 1827 and although it closed briefly for a period in the 1950s it reopened and remains a thriving place of worship today .

Hider postcard c1930, Uploders (West) looking towards Yondover with Boarsbarrow Hill in the distance. Top left is Knowle Farm, a mixed farm with a few dairy cows, pigs, chickens and ducks. The fields are now part of Higher Yondover Farm.

West View (Killick Cottage)

(Left) The picture taken from the field across the road shows the cottages and double gates in about 1920. At that time the gardens of the cottages included all the land now occupied by the three bungalows to the west. Agnes Crabb holds the hand of her niece, Annie Hawker (Paull).

(Above) In 1933, Annie Hawker, (later Paull), stands outside her home, West View with her new Rudge Whitworth bicycle ready to cycle to work having left school aged 14.

(Left) West View with its well in the foreground. The well supplied water to "West View" and later to the two bungalows that were built in the 1930s.

Budd's Cott (Rustic Glen)

'Aunt Ellen' stands at the door. The bungalow was later occupied by Mr and Mrs Eveleigh the parents of May who became the wife of Albert (Tubby) Wells and ran the Loders Post Office. I recall fairly regular chimney fires at Budd's Cott. The story was that this was how Mr Eveleigh cleaned his chimney; unsubstantiated but believable! This bungalow was built in the late 1920s next to Myrtle Cottage on land previously part of the garden of West View (now Killick Cottage). West View was then the home of George Marsh (my great-grandfather) and family.

Myrtle Cottage (formerly Temperance Cottage)

Bessie Wheeler at the front door. Was this once two houses? The house is set at right angles to the road and is very similar in alignment and appearance to others in the village. In the early 1900s Temperance Cottage was the home of Miss Willoughby who was warden at Uploders Methodist Chapel for many years.

Shatcombe House

Miss Stroud and her niece, Sarah Platt, outside the front door of Shatcombe House, (5 Shatcombe) where they lived.

During improvement works in 1994 the name Crabb 1898 was found inscribed on one of the roof timbers. Mr Ted Crabb (below, right) was the village carpenter and the date was, presumably, when the house was built. The layout and appearance of the houses at Shatcombe is similar to those between the School and New Street Lane in Loders and those at Newfoundland, Bradpole. It is very likely they were designed by the same architect or built by the same builder, or perhaps both?

Below is an extract from the Bridport News in December 1926. Mrs E.L. Hawker was my grandmother Emily Louisa Hawker. She purchased Shatcombe House on 22 December 1926 for £440. The wage for a working man then was about 40 shillings (£2) a week. The price paid was just over four times the annual earnings and although compared with today, appears to be a good deal the disposable income in 1920s would have been far less than it is today.

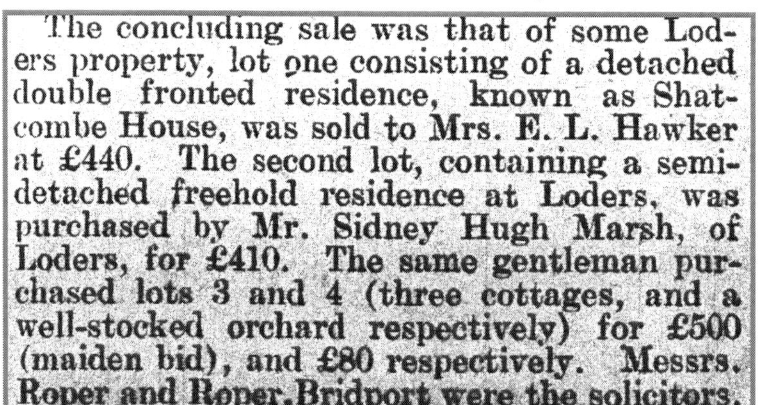

The concluding sale was that of some Loders property, lot one consisting of a detached double fronted residence, known as Shatcombe House, was sold to Mrs. E. L. Hawker at £440. The second lot, containing a semi-detached freehold residence at Loders, was purchased by Mr. Sidney Hugh Marsh, of Loders, for £410. The same gentleman purchased lots 3 and 4 (three cottages, and a well-stocked orchard respectively) for £500 (maiden bid), and £80 respectively. Messrs. Roper and Roper, Bridport were the solicitors.

Shatcombe

The name Shatcombe is derived from an old English word meaning a valley where sheep are kept; a clue to how it was many centuries ago.

The residents pose on the dirt road outside their houses on a sunny summer day in the early 1900s. This was the original terrace of three not long after they were built. There was a lean-to between number 3 and Shatcombe House.

About 30 years later, the lean-to has been demolished and number 4 built.

Yondover

Loders from Uploders taken across the road on the way to Yondover. The Ex-Servicemen's Hut is on the left, the Old Mill and the New Street Lane railway bridge are on the right. Lower Loders is in the distance.

Yondover looking south-westwards across New Street Lane and the Asker with distinctive conical shape of Boarsbarrow Hill in the distance. The cluster of buildings were, at one time, mostly associated with the local farms.

The Ex-Servicemen's Hut

The corrugated iron Ex -Servicemen's Hut was built at Yondover in 1926 by voluntary labour under the supervision of Mr F Fooks builder and son of the Headmaster of Loders School. Sir Edward Le Breton of Loders Court donated the land on which the hut was built. (Left) Mr Fooks(?) standing in the newly completed timber framework.

Initially it housed a skittle alley and games room. However, it soon became the centre of village activity with dances, socials, whist drives and concerts. It was also the regular meeting place for the Parish Council, the Women's Institute, the Mothers Union, the Youth Club, the Askerswell Young Farmers.

The Ex-Servicemen's Club closed in 1959 and the Hut was given to the village and renamed The Village Hall. But to many of the village people it fondly remained 'The Hut'. In 1972, the old Parish Room in New Road next to the Crown was sold for £3,750. The money raised was used to improve the Village Hall. The recently provided public sewer enabled modern flush toilets to be provided. The kitchen was modernised, as well as improved heating and lighting.

The two pictures on the next page were taken towards the end of the 1990s about the time I was the Parish Clerk. In hot weather the hut could get like an oven, in cold weather like a fridge! Before Parish Council meetings on cold winter evenings I arrived early to set up the room and pop a handful of 50p pieces into the electricity meter and turn on the wall mounted electric fan heaters. At the meetings everyone went suitably wrapped up but one of the Councillors, mindful of the likely temperature, would arrive with a hot water bottle as well as several layers of clothing. On the plus side, the discomfort concentrated the mind so the meetings tended to be short and to the point!

In 2000, after much hard work from John Hyde, Jessie Barrett and their team of willing helpers, a successful Lottery Grant application and much fund raising provided the money for our lovely new village hall on a different site on land generously given by Lord Hood of Loders Court.

When the Hut was replaced by the new Village Hall it had undoubtably outlived its useful life but, for over 70 years, it had provided a friendly meeting place for the village and its many organisations, activities and events. Its demolition was viewed with just a little sadness. To me it was, and always will be, the Hut.

The Ex-Servicemen's Hut - Later The Village Hall

These two pictures were taken in about 1998 towards the end of the life of the old Hut. At this time it was painted green; before that it was brown which was probably its original colour.

The interior of the Hut looking from the kitchen and stage end towards the entrance. Inside the front door was a short passageway with ladies' and gents' toilets to left and right respectively.

Higher Yondover Farm

The Hansford family and helpers haymaking in the 1920s or 1930s. The grass was cut in the fields, turned to dry, gathered loose as hay and built in to hayricks. The hay provided food for the cattle during the winter months.

On the right is Higher Yondover Farm thought to be in the 1950s when George Randall was the farmer. Once again, a hayrick is under construction.

Yondover

Martha Crabb with her children Hilda (Sis), David and Wilfred outside Yondover Cottages c1910. David became head gardener at Loders Court. Only their cottage had a door opening onto the road, all of the cottages do now.

(Left) Mrs Walter Bishop, the farmers wife, at the front door of Yondover Farmhouse. The house is on the inside of the sharp corner which was known locally as 'Bishop's Corner', named after the Bishops who lived on the corner.

(Left) Mr Walter Bishop, the Farmer on horseback at Yondover Farm.

Yondover - 'Bishops Corner'

Hider photograph looking from the corner eastwards. Yondover Farm and its barn are in the foreground with the farm buildings of Higher Yondover Farm in the distance. Bottom right is the stream which issues from the stone chute in the bank about 50 yards along the road. It supplied cool clear drinking water to the nearby cottages and to passers-by on hot days. The stream was piped in about 1960 enabling the road to be slightly widened.

Potts of Bridport postcard from about 1930. Yondover Farm is on the right. Brook House, facing, with the stream in front of it is now a much larger property.

Fire at Yondover 28 June 1921

(Taken from the Bridport News 1st July 1921.
Pictures by Potts of Bridport)

LODERS BARN AND COTTAGE DESTROYED IN FIRE EXCITING SCENES

The peaceful quietude of this little West Dorset village was suddenly disturbed on Friday evening when a fire was discovered in a barn belonging to Mr Harold Bishop. Just before 9 o'clock PC Jones and several other villagers noticed smoke issuing from the building, and they immediately hastened to the spot. A quantity of straw outside the building had become ignited, and the roof of the barn inside was in flames. A message was dispatched to Bridport summoning the Fire Brigade who

lately arrived in charge of Mr HH Hounsell. In the meantime, the inhabitants worked assiduously in throwing buckets of water on the burning thatch and saturating the roof of two cottages standing within 20 yards of the barn.

The fire had obtained such a hold that when the Brigade arrived on the scene it was found that nothing could be done to save the barn. The combined efforts of the Brigade and the villagers were there-upon directed in preventing the fire from spreading. Sparks were flying in all directions, but fortunately no further damage was caused. The barn was completely gutted, and most of the agricultural implements that had been stored there were destroyed. The damage is roughly estimated at £350. A word of praise is due to the villagers for the splendid manner in which they worked under the direction of PC Bown and PC Jones.

A further outbreak of fire occurred in the village on Tuesday evening, resulting in a total disruption of three cottages, the property of Mr Harold Bishop. These were situated at the rear of Mr Walbridge's farmhouse, standing in a row under one thatched roof. Early in the evening a flame was seen rising from the ridge of the roof over the centre cottage which happened to be unoccupied and within a short space of time the roof was ablaze. People quickly flocked to the scene of the conflagration and efforts were made to remove the contents of the two other cottages, occupied by Mr Crabb and Mrs Burbidge, an elderly lady.

The prompt action of Mr Walter Samways, a foreman porter on the GWR in coming to the assistance of Mrs Crabb, who lay ill, suffering from the shock experienced in the last fire, is worthy of the highest praise. Although the building was burning fiercely he managed to bring her through unscathed. In her weakened state, the fright rendered her unconscious and medical aid had to be requisitioned. Mindful of the plight of Mrs Burbidge, a labourer, Walter Hansford, entered the cottage and she, too, was helped to safety.

Pictures of the fire and the crowd taken from near Yondover Farmhouse. New House Farm is on the left and the stream that once ran alongside the road can be seen in the bottom picture.

Furniture was piled high in the lane, everyone worked with a will, and altogether it was an exceedingly exciting time. The Bridport Fire Brigade, who had been apprised of the outbreak arrived and at once set to work in preventing further damage to adjoining property from the first there was no possibility of saving the cottages, the fire, to use the words of an onlooker "spreading like lightning".

Pictures showing the Goods and Chattels stacked in Barr Lane.

All three cottages were completely burnt out, the estimated damage being in the region of £300.

Seeing there was no fire in any of the cottages at the time, it is supposed that a spark from some adjoining building must have fallen on the roof, and the thatch being dry, quickly became alight.

As on the previous occasion valuable assistance was rendered by Sergeant Bown of Bridport and PC Jones.

We understand that the barn and cottages are insured.

Fire at Yondover July 1909

Photograph taken from the Bridport to Maiden Newton railway embankment showing a steam driven fire engine pumping water from the River Asker. The fire was on 2 July 1909 and the card was posted at 3.45pm on 8 July 1909. This card was rescued from a bonfire. The family of an old lady who has passed away were throwing a lot of old papers on a bonfire. Mrs Peck who lived at Myrtle Cottage was helping, spotted the card and said, "I expect Mrs Paull (my mother) would be interested in that". She was and eventually passed it to me. I often wonder what other treasures were burnt on that day!

The photographer leant over the bridge parapet to take this one. The fire, judging by the smoke, appears to be around the corner. People had travelled by foot, bicycle and pony and trap. By the time the picture was taken the crowd seem to have lost interest in the fire.

The Bridport to Maiden Newton Branch Line

The Bridport Railway opened on 12 November 1857 and closed in May 1975. The construction of this impressive feat of Civil Engineering must have had a big impact on the village. A site base was set up in Loders and it was here that the first sod was cut by Joseph Gundry on 19 June 1855. In Loders, as well as the major earthworks, three bridges and a cattle creep were built over a distance of less than a quarter of a mile. At the end of the project on 20 November 1857 at Loders the contractors surplus equipment was sold including 25 horses, 30 earth wagons and 50 tons of contractor's rails. *(More information on the railway can be found in "The Bridport Railway" by BL Jackson and MJ Tattershall.)*

For over two years the site compound and the considerable number of men associated with the project lived and lodged around the village. I am sure that a number of them must have met the local young ladies and maybe married and settled in the village. Prior to 1857 the only means of transport was by foot or horseback so most of the inhabitants of Loders had probably travelled only as far as Bridport or other neighbouring villages. Dorchester would have been out of reach for most people. Suddenly with a short journey to Bridport or Powerstock stations there was access to anywhere in the country.

In 1940 a gun-siding for a 12-inch Howitzer gun was constructed alongside the railway in Loders. It and a similar siding in Bradpole were removed in 1945. In May 1947, the Ministry of Transport confirmed that the provision of a halt at Loders had been approved in principal but it got no further. In the 1960s and 70s the passenger numbers dwindled to such an extent that it was no longer viable to keep the line open. The trains often ran almost empty.

(Above) The railway sweeps through Loders on a smooth curve with bridges over the Asker, the road at Yondover and New Street Lane. The once cultivated garden between the railway and New Street Lane is clearly visible. The large field left of the railway is now the site of the Cemetery, the allotments and Highacres.

A tank engine with two carriages travels towards Maiden Newton on the stretch of railway line east of Loders, just past the allotments. This is typical of the types of train that ran on the line in the 1950s. A wave to the driver by the bridge at Yondover was always reciprocated.

A single car diesel unit in the cutting just below the Cemetery and the allotments on 26 April 1976. These units were employed on the branch line from the late 1960s until the closure of the line in 1975. They were more than adequate to cope with the passenger numbers. At times, they ran virtually empty.

For people living in Loders there was a choice of two railway stations. Bridport Station (left in the 1950s) was the choice of most. It was a short easy journey along roads by bus, taxi, bike or on foot. For some, particularly at the eastern end of Uploders, the station at Powerstock was an alternative. It was the nearest but to reach it meant a walk of some one and a half miles across fields by way of farm tracks and footpaths. The tracks were well made from locally quarried stone but were uneven and became muddy in wet weather. They must have been particularly difficult in the dark winter evenings for the half hour, or so, walk across country.

Left, Powerstock Station as it was in the 1930s with wagons in the siding. The railway on the left is the Maiden Newton to Bridport line looking towards Bridport (and, of course, Loders!).

Although the line did not close until 1975 Powerstock Station was sold by British Rail to Brian and Diana Read in 1968. They carried out extensive works to convert the old station to a comfortable dwelling for themselves and their two children, Giles and Rosie. *(See Powerstock Station - All Change by Diana P Read).*

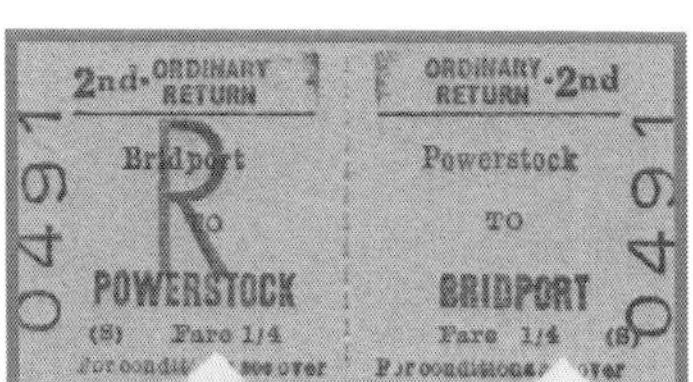

An unissued return ticket from Bridport to Powerstock from the 1960's. The return fare was 1s4d (one shilling and four pence) which is just under seven pence in today's currency.

New Street Lane - Yondover Farm, Farm Workers

Farm workers with a steam traction engine probably from Yondover Farm. The barn is believed to be the one at the west end of New Street Lane which was converted in to a house in the 1990s. The man, front centre, holding a flask and mug is better dressed than the rest so is probably the Farmer.

Farm workers with Shire horses in New Street Lane. The house is Mudlark, a thatched cottage before it was extended and modernised. These men are also thought to be from Yondover Farm. The man on the horse on the right could be the same as the one on the traction engine in the driver's position.

New Street Lane

(Left) A view over Yondover from Boarsbarrow with New Street Lane in the distance. The white house is Mudlark. Just to the right of Mudlark is the old cottage which in the 1950s was a ruin with no roof just crumbling walls and so a good place to explore and play! The houses are better seen in the enlargement (left, below).

New Street Lane is believed to be on the route of the Roman Road from Eggardon to Exeter. Examination of small-scale Ordnance Survey maps confirms the possibility of this being the case.

The village is said to have once been located on New Street Lane but was relocated due to an outbreak of the plague in the 1300s. Had that not happened Uploders would, perhaps, now be located along New Street Lane at the foot of the south facing hillside; an interesting thought .

The Old Mill where the old wheel still turns. The mill ground corn and probably flax. It was a bolling-mill. The pounding machinery of the bolling-mill would have pounded the stalks of flax which was grown nearby.

Lower Loders (now known as Loders)

Lower Loders is the most westerly part of the village. With the Court, the Church, the School, two pubic houses and the village policeman it might have once considered itself to be the most important part of the village, something that would have been hotly disputed by the residents of Uploders and Yondover!

Lower Loders from the Church in the west to east of the school as viewed from south of Yondover. The Maiden Newton Railway runs south of the village and In the foreground (bottom right) is the western end of Yondover.

The summer evening sun shining over the village illuminates the strip-lynchets on Waddon Hill. The photograph shows Loders from the Farmers Arms on the left to the School on the right. The thatched cottages to the left of the Loders Arms have long since disappeared and is now the seating area outside the pub. The card was published by Shephard, Bridport, c1905.

Near the School

Card posted in 1932; the man with the stick is thought to be Frank Greening. The door in the wall on the left is to the old pump house that provided water to the nearby houses. The pump house was removed in 1975 when Smishops Lane was widened as a condition of the Highacres development. The well remains in the garden of Smishops. The houses on the right have hardly changed. A horse drawn delivery cart can just be seen at the end of the road, probably that of Mr Macey who lived in the house on the corner. Long after Mr Macey had gone this corner was known to the villagers as Macey's Corner.

A crowd at the hunt meet outside Loders School. Amongst the riders is Harold Bishop, the third horse rider from the left. The lady at the back, between the door and window, with her hands clasped is Mrs Hettie Crabb.

Loders School

(Above) Believed to be the opening in 1869. Sir Molyneaux and Lady Nepean appear not to be in the picture, no one looks grand enough. The postcard cannot be contemporaneous with the opening. The first picture postcards were produced in 1894 and divided back cards (which this one is) followed in 1902. It is possible that the cards were produced from a plate from 1869 for a special event or anniversary in 1902, or later. Alternatively, it could be a re-enactment of the opening in the early 1900s. It is one of the few family pictures with no details on the back. My grandmother, Emily Marsh (Hawker), was born in 1892 so would have been a pupil here between 1897 and 1905. Maybe it was an event when she was a pupil. I prefer to think it is a picture from an 1869 plate. Who knows?

Extract from the Bridport News 15 October 1869

OPENING OF THE LODERS SCHOOL

The little village of Loders was on Wednesday the scene of much public festivity on the occasion of the opening of the new schools (sic) which have recently been erected there for the benefit of the parish. For many years the want of adequate accommodation for the children of the parish desirous of participating in scholastic benefits has been keenly felt , but until lately the matter was not practically dealt with. Lady Nepean of Loders Court, impressed with the desirability of such a building being raised, resolved to erect at her sole cost a new school-room as a substitute for the old building formerly used; and in this munificent determination she was most cordially seconded by her husband. Sir Molyneaux Nepean, Bart., Lord of the Manor at Loders. Accordingly without delay, operations were commenced. A site, admirably suited for the building , was given by Sir Molyneaux, and early in the present year the foundation stone of the new school was laid by her ladyship, and no effort was spared for the speedy completion of the work……...The School had been prettily decorated for the occasion, so the appearance which it presented was singularly pleasing. Outside the porch were temporarily planted several magnificent fir trees and over the door there was a small arch formed of evergreens and flowers.

From 1869 to 1918 the School catered for children from the ages of 5 to 12 or 13. In 1918 the school leaving age increased to 14. Those who were able to win a scholarship or whose parents could afford it transferred to Bridport Grammar School. The majority did not. They left school at the relevant leaving age to start work and, in many cases, follow in their parents' footsteps .

View across the road from the plot that is now the garden of Smishops showing the school in about 1930. The school flagpole and the porches on the houses have gone. Otherwise the street scene is almost unchanged..

The children seem in happy mood, perhaps it is the end of term? The group of boys stand on the wall of what is now Smishops. A wicket gate leads from the road to the field with a new haystack in the top corner. The door to the old pump house is at the right hand end of the wall. Water for the school and nearby houses would have been fetched from there in buckets.

The teachers and pupils on the road outside the school. They are from the left:- (Back) Miss Hockey, Barbara Brown, Ivy Hansford, Freda Godden, Violet Hyde, Enid Crabb, Ivy Gill, Amy Symes, George Crabb; (Middle) Donald Brown, -?-, -?-, Chubb, F Hansford, Jack Pullman, H Crabb, Frank Crabb, Bill Gill, Blanche Knight, Miss Read; (Front) F Brown, ? Chubb, William Symes, Jack Gale, Bertha Symes, --?- , -?- ,David Hyde, M Hansford, -?-, Vera Knight, -?-.

Loders School children in 1924 dancing around the maypole, a tradition re-introduced in recent years. (Left to right) Doris Ward, Ronald Legg, Bertha Symes, Fred Read, Clara Ward, Fred Darby, Lily Peach, George Hyde, Lily Samways, George Fooks, May Hudson, Roy Richards, Linda Brown, Bill Symes, Louise Hudson and Percy Read. The card is by Percy S. Smith of Bridport.

Miss Hinks with the infants in 1925. They are from the left (back) Jack Crabb, Walter Bishop, Bill Budden, Vera Read, Margery Dawe, Ethel Ward, Winnie Coombs, Edgar Bishop, Linda Baker (Harper). (Middle) Dorothy Read (Broom) Eileen Read, Violet Richards, Ernie Symes, Elizabeth Read, Letty Darby.
(Front) P Hansford and Pearl Gale (Symes).

Senior pupils with their teacher, Miss Garland, in about 1930. From the left:- (back) Victor Darby, Teddy Pitcher, Sidney Coombs, Tom Norman, Kenneth Fowler. (Middle) Freda Powell, Alice Rogers, Mary Aliss, Dora Paul (Hyde), Vera Legg, Vera Rendell. (Front) Mabel Symes (Skeats), Ethel Ward, Winnie Read (Ward), Annie Hawker (Paull), Ruby Richards and May Sanders.

17 Loders and Westwards

17 Loders has a stone by the porch dated 1755. It was once two cottages.
To its left is 18 Loders. This was set at a right angle to the road with its front door off a side path and not off the main street. In the 1960s it was demolished and a new house built in the gap between 19 and 17. The last occupant was Minnie Crabb, the fortune teller. Although we local children were rather nervous of her and her mystic powers her regular clients swore by her predictions. As long as she told them what they wanted to hear; which, I'm lead to believe, she generally did.

Picture printed by Roger Pinn from a Hider glass plate. It was taken from outside the school, probably in the early 1950s. Two cyclists head westwards, possibly to Bridport for work or shopping. Not many had cars then. The bicycle was the most convenient way to go to 'town'. Electricity and telephones had well and truly arrived, the skyline is criss-crossed with wires, now, thankfully removed. The thatch on the roof of 19 has a covering of galvanised corrugated iron.

19 Loders and Nearby

George Read outside his house, 19 Loders, c1920, chatting to a man on a bike. This side of 19 is the adjoining cottage, 18 Loders.

The picture below dates from about 1918 showing Kate Read (my mother's aunt) with three of her children, Aggie, Ivy and Percy. Edna and Eileen came later. Aggie moved to Cheltenham, married and became the owner of a successful grocery shop. Ivy moved to London, Percy to Yeovil, Edna to Beaminster and Eileen also to London.

I was fairly young when Aunt Kate died. My memories are of a highly polished house with a wooden high backed-chair and a stuffed animal of some variety. I can remember Kate talking about her 'Buddery Door' apples. Many years later I discovered they were Buttery D'Or. Apparently they are sharp apples for cooking and cider making and they come from Dorset. I wonder, if the tree is still there?

As an aside, collecting postcards can lead to some chance encounters. When I was about 10 we stayed with Ivy and her family in London during the summer holidays and became friendly with a nearby relative, Roger. Some 55 years later my wife, Christine, and I were at a postcard fair at the Royal Horticultural Halls in London where we found a couple of Loders postcards. One showed 19 Loders. We were talking about this when the man next to us joined in and told us that he had stayed at number19 with Aunt Kate. It turned out he was Roger's brother.

From the School to the Loders Arms

Most likely one of the village's several carriers making his way slowly along the street on a sunny summer day. In 1927, Kelly's Directory listed the following carriers for Loders:- J Macey and Son; Stephen Crabb; Sidney Allis and Ernest Watts daily to Bridport and Steven Crabb to Weymouth on Fridays.

On a hot summer day Mr Tolley (left) standing outside the doorway of Waddon Farmhouse (The Barns). This 17th century farmhouse was extended in the 18th century and again more recently. On the right, Judy Greening stands in her front porch. In the distance one of the village carriers is delivering to the Loders Arms.

Fire at 41 Loders September 1929

Taken from the Bridport News 4th October 1929

Tragic Occurrence at Loders.
Respected Inhabitant's Untimely Death
Fell Down Stairs During Fire

The little village of Loders was plunged in gloom on Saturday afternoon when one of its most respected and popular residents lost his life, in distressing circumstances.

A serious fire had broken out in a row of outbuildings attached to the Loders Arms, the licensee of which is Mrs Flora Richards and the building being thatched, the flames quickly rose to a great height and threatened to spread to an adjoining thatched cottage where lived Mr Frederick Fooks aged about 47, his wife, two children and an invalid sister.

Mr Fooks who was a carpenter and joiner, at once set to work removing furniture from the dwelling as a precaution, and it was while thus engaged that he fell down a flight of stairs, breaking his neck. Death was practically instantaneous.

Among the crowd watching the fire fighting are Hilda Greening, second left, talking to someone at the door or window. Mr. Ellery (nearest with his hands behind his back) and David and Nellie Crabb (Jessie (Barrett) and David's parents) near the front with their hands on their hips.

When they heard of Mr Fooks' death villagers who had turned out to help watched the procession as the body was removed with tears in their eyes, for he was one of the most well-liked men in the village. He was Secretary of the Loders branch of Oddfellows, while he took a deep interest in the affairs of the church.

Bridport Fire Brigade made a prompt response under Chief Officer G L Atherton, and eventually succeeded in getting the fire under control. The conflagration was confined to the outbuildings, which consisted of milking sheds and a carpenter's shop.

The inquest: *An inquiry into the circumstances attending the fatality was held at Loders Arms on Monday afternoon by the Deputy Coroner for West Dorset (Mr S Edgar Howard) . PC Sartin, Bridport acted as Coroner .*

The first witness called was Mr Henry John Fooks of 18 St. Andrews Road, Bridport. He identified the body as, that of his brother, William Frederick Fooks who resided at No 41 Loders. Deceased was a carpenter by trade and enjoyed quite normal health. To the witness's knowledge he had never had a day's illness. His age was 47.

Sidney George Hyde, 20 Loders, said he was present 5 minutes after the fire had broken out in some outbuildings attached to the Loders Arms. Deceased's house was adjoining the scene of the outbreak. He (witness) assisted Mr Fooks to remove his furniture. One corner of the deceased's residence had caught alight. There was no smoke in the house at the time of the accident, witness and others having closed the window.

Continuing witness said that no one actually saw the accident. He and Mrs Fooks were engaged removing a mirror, which would not go down the stairs. Deceased got a screw-driver, loosened the two screws, and then dropped the screwdriver. He (deceased) then proceeded down the stairs with one part of the mirror and witness followed behind a couple of seconds later. When he (witness) came to the top of the stairs he saw deceased lying at the bottom. He heard no cry or fall. It was a straight staircase. As soon as witness saw deceased he ran down the stairs. The mirror deceased had been carrying was half-way down the stairs, Mr Fooks was lying on his back with his feet up the stairs. Witness and a neighbour Mr Ward, carried Mr Fooks into the roadway. Deceased showed no signs of life.

Thomas George Kimber Ward, 2 Yondover, said he was helping to remove the furniture from the house. He was on the ground floor at the time of the accident and a yard or so away from the foot of the stairs, suddenly he heard a crash and turning round he saw Mr Fooks lying at the foot of the stairs in the manner described by the previous witness. He (witness) raised Mr Fooks' head but there were no signs of life. Artificial respiration was applied for about 20 minutes but all to no purpose.

Dr Sanctuary, Bridport who was sent for, announced that Mr Fooks' neck was broken. Stanley Tolley of Waddon House, Loders who said he also was present at the fire, deposed to assisting to carry deceased from the house. He heard the doctor say that deceased had broken his neck.

In returning a verdict of accidental death, the deputy coroner said it was a most lamentable accident which they all deplored. He tendered sincere sympathy with the members of deceased's family.

Mrs Flora Richards, licensee of the Loders Arms and the witnesses gave their fees to the widow. "It would have been preferred by far had the house and furniture been destroyed than that we should have lost a man like Mr Fooks was the comment of Dr Ward, one of the witnesses, which concurred with the Deputy Coroner's expressions of sympathy with the widow and other members of the family.

Scenes at the funeral: *Many members of Oddfellows, ex servicemen and a large representation of the general public attended the funeral, which took place on Tuesday at Loders Parish Church burial ground. As the funeral procession wended its way through the village from Waddon Farm, the house of Mr Tolley, where the body had been reposed since Saturday, tributes of respect were paid by the inhabitants among whom were those who had known the deceased as a merry, carefree boy and later as a bluff good natured man, whose cheerfulness and sunny disposition had often been the means of lightening to a sorrow borne by his fellows.*

The coffin was covered with floral tributes, while the majority of those walking in the procession carried wreaths and other such expressions of sympathy.

The cortêge was met at the entrance to the churchyard by the vicar Rev A.B. Hutton (pictured right) who preceded it into the church, where many of the village woman folk and other friends of deceased had assembled. There a short but impressive service was conducted by the Vicar, who afterwards performed the last sad rites at the graveside.

The Loders Arms

Card posted on 31 December 1908 showing the landlord and his family, thought to be the Hudsons, outside the pub. The wagon in the foreground is one of the village carriers, possibly Mr Macey or Mr Woodrow. The other wagon carries coal collected from Bridport Station and loaded into hundredweight (51kg) hessian sacks for delivery. Quite an eventful day in the village!

A later postcard, c1934; a car waits outside Number 41. On the right, Mary Alice stands by the front doorstep talking to three small children, the Rogers family. Mrs Symes, the carpenter's wife, stands in the doorway of her thatched cottage beyond the pub. This is long since gone and is now part of the garden at the Loders Arms. The carrier, Mr Macey (?), is watched by two small boys. The late Bill Budden thought they were probably his brother, Tony, and him.

Loders Arms to The Farmers Arms

There are a number of postcards of this short section of road. At first glance they are all very similar but they do show the changes over 50 or 60 years.

Card dating from the early 1900s published by W&E Frost, Bridport. On the left are the cottages next to the Loders Arms, now long gone. The little girl is thought to be Sarah Read. Although the street scene appears little different from today nearly all the houses behind the little girl on her side of the road have been replaced with new ones set back from the pavement.

About 30 years later taken from outside the Loders Arms (left). A couple of cars are parked on the street and the cottages next to the pub are still standing.

Picture taken c1930 by Claude Hider showing Mrs Budden's shop. The street appears to be surfaced, the stains on the surfacing show evidence of passing livestock, probably delivery horses that had to stand and wait. Several of the thatched roofs have a covering of corrugated iron. This was once a fairly common feature. It was cheaper than re-thatching.

One of Claude Hider's later cards showing the shop and sign which reads 'The Old Shop, Established 1896'. The corrugated iron sheeting has been removed and replaced with pristine thatch most likely laid by Sam Legg, the village thatcher. The house boasts a new porch and electricity and the telephone have arrived so it must be 1936, or later.

Loders Post Offices

Until the late 1930s, 27 Loders was a Post Office (PO) and Greengrocers run by the Postmistress, Mrs Budden. This has been demolished and replaced with a bungalow. In the late 1930s Mrs Wells became the Postmistress in the shop and Post Office at 38 Loders, just across the road from Number 27. The picture, above, shows the sign to Mrs Budden's PO and shop on the right. The house in the foreground (left) is 38 Loders which became the home of the Wells family. The single storey building was the Post Office and Store until 1992.

The handstamp (right) **LOWER LODERS BRIDPORT**, was applied to a postcard most probably by Mrs Budden, in the original Loders PO on 21 August 1911.

The cancellations (above) **LODERS BRIDPORT DORSET**, were applied at the Loders PO, 38 Loders, on the 29 January 1966, in all probability by Mrs May Wells, the Postmistress who is pictured right.

The Farmers Arms

The Farmers Arms from a postcard c1910 with the Loders Arms in the distance. The landlord and landlady of the pub, Mr and Mrs Blackler, stand at the corner.

Electricity came to the village in 1936 so this must have been later, probably the 1940s. The Blackler's daughter married Mr Pitcher, who became the next landlord. The lady by the door could be Mrs Pitcher. The others look like visitors.

The Farmers Arms with the Loders Arms in the distance c1930. The cottages beside the Loders Arms are long-gone, replaced with a car park and later an outside seating area. In the distance on the left is Mr Budden's shop with its sign above and to the left of the car parked outside.

East and West of Church Farm

Photograph taken in about 1934 with Church Farm house on the left and the Loders Arms in the distance. A group of people stand outside Mrs Budden's shop; the children quite likely include Bill and Tony Budden.

Looking west from near the Farmers Arms c1910. The building on the near left was the pony shed for the pub. It no longer exists. Where it once stood is now part of the paved area in front of the Farmers Arms. The old barn built on the inside of the corner by the church is visible to the right of the church gate. In the foreground on the right are the Church Farm buildings.

Church Farm

Mrs Ivy Crabb stands at the front of Church Farmhouse in about 1925. The sign 'Motor for Hire' refers to the cars belonging to Mr Ernest Watts, the taxi driver and car hirer who worked from the yard beside Church Farmhouse. This area is now occupied by Church Farm Cottage.

(Left) Mr Crabb outside the house also in the mid-1920s. He is dressed as a farmer and other workers did in those days. In the 1950s many still wore similar clothing, a shirt with a detachable stud collar (usually not attached), a weskit (waistcoat), heavy trousers, hobnailed boots and a trilby hat.

The West-end of Lower Loders

Card posted in 1905. The houses on the south, right-hand, side remain largely unchanged to this day. On the north side the old houses were later demolished and replaced with new ones set back slightly from the road. Parts of the front walls of the old houses were left to act as retaining walls to the new houses. The furthest of the two new houses served as a police station in the 1950s.

Picture taken in about 1934 from a similar position as the card above. New houses have replaced the old cottages. Children of the Farnham family peer over the wall that was once part of the old cottages. Along the street is a motorbike and side-car, possibly Mr Osborne's. This was a popular mode of transport for families at this time with mum clinging on the back of the motorbike and the children or maybe granny in the sidecar!

Extract from an unused card by Potts of Bridport dating from the early 1900s taken on a sunny summer day from a very similar position as the pictures on the previous page. There is a good gathering of people, presumably outside their own houses. They are mainly women and children so it was probably taken on a weekday when the men were at work.

The 1937 Coronation
13 May 1937, 28a Loders is decorated for the Coronation of King George VI. Kate, Elsie Nellie and Agnes Hansford stand in front of their decorated house.

As mentioned on the previous page, these houses replaced those in the picture above.

The West End of the Village

A faded postcard; flags and a banner across the road by the Vicarage which reads 'THE PARISH WELCOMES YOU RIGHT HEARTILY'. It could be the end of the Great War in 1918 or the end of the Boer War in 1902.

Loders End opposite Loders Court c1930. The three Hinks sisters, who are thought to be in the picture, lived in the middle of the three cottages. Their father was Coachman for Lady Nepean at Loders Court. The sisters attended Loders School and Elizabeth went on to teach the infants there for 40 years. Edith did domestic service in South Africa and Malta before being with Lady Le Breton at the Court for 23 years. They moved to Frome Vauchurch in 1958 to share a bungalow with Mrs Harvey who was once in service with Edith at Loders Court.

Views of the West End of Loders

Published by Hine Bros., Bridport c1910 showing the west end of the village. In the foreground is the Bridport to Maiden Newton Railway. The parapets of the little brick cattle-creep can just about be seen to the right of the bushes. Just beyond the railway is the River Asker with a footbridge crossing into the orchard.

West end of village showing the Church, Loders Court, the Vicarage and the rear of houses along the village street. The lane that runs from the village street past the Vicarage and Garden Cottage can be clearly seen. Neat rows of vegetables, potatoes perhaps, in the gardens on an early summer evening.

Loders Court, the Church and the Vicarage

These are all located at the west end of Loders. The Court is on the site of a Priory founded by the Abbot of Montebourg by a Charter granted in 1108. In 1414 Henry V decreed that all foreign monasteries in England be dissolved. Following this the Priory became a farmhouse and later the manor house..

From the left, the Church of St Mary Magdalene, the Court and the Vicarage in about 1920. The eastern end of the Court was demolished in 1969.

The footbridges over the river and millstream link the footpath from the north side of Boarsbarrow to the village alongside the Vicarage. Someone is hanging out washing near the big tree so maybe the photograph was taken on a Monday, the traditional washing day. The card by R D Barrett was posted in 1906.

The Vicarage (Now Loders Hall)

The rear of the Vicarage in the early part of the 1900s. The Vicar from 1887 to 1914 was David Thomas. A lady in Edwardian dress, the Vicar's wife Mrs Thomas perhaps and her dog are sitting on the seat on the lawn.

Sunday School group on the Vicarage lawn with the Reverend Hutton who is standing at the back gazing away from the camera. He was the Vicar of Loders from 1914 to 1935. The little girl on the left, in the second row from the front is thought to be Annie Hawker (Paull), my mother. If so it would be about 1924.

Loders Sunday School during the Second World War

Even though the country was at war some life continued much as normal .

The older Loders Sunday School children on the Vicarage lawn in about 1942. (Back from left) Margaret Darby, -?- (evacuee). Dennis Yarde and Phillip Symes. (Middle standing), -?-, -?-, Mrs Palmer and Queenie Carr (evacuee). (Sitting), Doreen Watts, Jessie Crabb (Barrett), Kenny Eddison, -?- (evacuee), Avril Greening, Margaret Bourne (head down), Jean Rogers (Cornish) and Peggie

The younger members of the Sunday School with the Reverend Beardmore, Miss Hinks the infants' teacher, and Miss Vera Legg at the Vicarage.

St Mary Magdalene's Church

The Church, built in the local limestone, dates from the 11th century and has some Norman features. From 1107 to 1410 it was the church of the adjacent Priory. It was restored in the 19th century.

(Above) The Church from the east by the local Bridport photographer, Hare. The white headstone on the left is dated 1906 so the photograph must have been taken soon after then. Five well trimmed yew bushes line the pathway to the church. The oil lamp lit the path on dark Sunday evenings. Although unused they remained until the 2000s.

Harvest Festival

(Left) The Church decorated with flowers, fruit and vegetables for the Harvest Festival service. Oil lamps hang from the ceiling. Otherwise the interior remains largely unchanged from what it is today.

Interior of the Church prior to restoration in 1901 showing the box-pews. If you have ever sat in a box pew for more than a few minutes you will know they are not

comfortable! The lectern and ornate oil lamps are to the right of the pulpit.
This card, posted 7 August 1928, was probably from a scout, camping at Loders Court. He says, "I am writing the card while Mr Prior is taking kit inspection". The picture was taken from just inside the main door and shows the font, the pews,

The Reverend David Thomas with the ladies' choir outside the Church door c1908. From the left (back) Reverend Thomas, Millicent Crabb, Ella Randall, Frances Curtis, Jessie Brown, Gladys Blackler, Gladys Brown, Hilda Russell, Miss J Thomas. (Middle) R Gale, M Lee, E Budden, D Russell, B Samways.
(Front) M Crabb, E Hyde, M Read, A Pitcher, M Budden.

In 1933 a number of girls from Loders were confirmed at a Confirmation Service held at Bothenhampton Church. Those identified are;- (left) Mabel Symes (Skeats), (sixth) Annie Hawker (Paull). (First on right) Pearl Gale (Symes), (third) Winnie Read (Ward). Centre at the back is Doris Rowe, Keith Alner's mother.

Loders Court

Parliamentarian Denzil Holles, Earl of Clare, held the Manor when Charles II fled through the parish on his way from Bridport to Broadwindsor. In 1799 Sir Evan Nepean, former Governor of Bombay and Secretary of the Admiralty, purchased the estate and remoulded the house as it is shown below. Nelson is said to have stayed here several times with Sir Evan.

Viewed from the north c1935 showing the original Georgian building with its Victorian extension on the left. The latter was removed in 1969 thus returning The Court to its original and more pleasing Georgian proportions.

This garden is between the old east wing of the Court and the churchyard. The Church is on the left and the Court, as it was pre-1969, is on the right.

Loders Court and the Church viewed from the west. The picture, by Claud Hider, dates from c1930. The area between the road and the grazing, on the left, is a garden area. The Church tower is hidden behind the large horse-chestnut tree.

(Left) The Head Gardener David Crabb with Percy Darby, Alston Paul and Bill Saunders standing beside the recently constructed pond. It was one of several that ran down through the garden towards the river.

View from the Court looking towards the Vicarage, on the right, and beyond to the hills at Yondover.

Rehearsals at Loders Court c1893

These pictures below are all described on the backs as 'A Rehearsal in Loders Court Garden' for various Tableaux due to be held at Loders School. One of the cast is Mary Weldon who, on another picture, is described as daughter of the Reverend Weldon, Rector of Bridport, a position he held from 1891 to 1895.

(Left) The Italian Floral Dance arranged by Maria Chigi. Maria is second from the right,

At the time of the 1891 Census, Marchese Angelo Chigi of Siena, was at Loders Court and recorded as a great nephew of Sir Molyneux Nepean. On the deaths of Sir Molyneux and Lady Nepean, The Court passed to him as their closest surviving relative but he never took up residence.

Rehearsing for Sleeping Beauty are, from the left, G.G.Williams (Good Fairy) M.Cross (Nurse with Royal Baby) Maria Chigi (Queen) J.A.Williams (King), Agnes Cross (Bad Fairy). The corner of the Church tower can just be seen on the left of the picture.

Cinderella's Ball: E.F.Parkinson (Good Fairy), Maria Chigi (Princess Cinderella), F.Maunsell (Prince Charming), G.G.Williams and J.A.Williams (The Sour Sisters)

Loders Fête 1886 and 1908

The Fête is a social occasion to raise funds for the Church and other organisations in the Parish and Benefice. With the kind consent of the owners it has for many years been held in the grounds of Loders Court. The earliest reference to the Loders Fête appeared in the Bridport News in 1886.

BRIDPORT NEWS 11 JUNE 1886

THE FETE AND GALA AT LODERS — The first fete of the Nepean Lodge of Oddfellows, to be held on Whit-Monday, promises to be one of the best ever held in the neighbourhood. The members of the local Court of Foresters and the Great Western Lodge of Oddfellows (as will be seen in the advertisements in our column) have decided to join the brethren at Loders so that, unless the weather should unfortunately prove wet, there will be a large concourse of persons. The Bon-Bon Brothers, the marvellous high wire rope walkers, will give three performances, which will be quite a novelty in this neighbourhood. There are other attractions, including arrangements for dancing, and above all the beautiful grounds of Loders Court. Sir M. Nepean will preside, the vice-chair being occupied by Mr. W. Knight. A large attendance of both patrons and visitors is expected.

This postcard was posted on 24 October 1908 which means that this fête was in 1908, or earlier. At first glance it could be a recent fête. The location is the same, only the clothes have changed. The musicians and the crowd gather to watch an attraction on the lawn. All are dressed in their Sunday best. Quite a fashion display, the ladies in long frocks and picture hats and men in their best Sunday suits and hats. The card was sent to a Miss Cross in London. The message reads, “Many happy returns of the day. from Uncle”.

Entertainment at the 1908 Fête

These two cards and the one on the previous page are by the same publisher. They contain common features, for example the music stands, so it's a reasonable assumption that all were taken at the same event. Both show the well dressed and attentive audience watching a performance of Richard III as traditionally portrayed as a hunchback. The musicians (below, left) are having a well earned rest and enjoying the entertainment.

The 1926 Fête

Some of the fête pictures have '1926 Fete' on the backs so by comparing features in others they can also be identified as being from the 1926 fête. Several postcards from Keith Alner's collection have notes on the back stating 'Uploders Fête at Mr Lesser's Farms, Matravers'. Rather than being the site of the fête it is thought more likely that it was the gathering point for the procession starting at Matravers and finishing at Loders Court. There is supporting evidence for this from pictures taken along the journey .

Extract from the Western Gazette, August 1926

FETE AT LODERS COURT

FLOWER SHOW AND SPORTS - A RECORD ENTRY.

The annual Loders flower show and fête took place on Thursday, and was held in the picturesque grounds of Loders Court, kindly loaned for the occasion by Lieut. Colonel E.P. Le Breton.

The entries constituted a record, numbering no fewer than 185, upon which all concerned are to be congratulated. The arrangements were most satisfactory, the various events composing the long and well varied programme being got through with dispatch.

The Tea Committee comprised Mesdames Tolley, W. Hansford, Williams, J. Hansford, Samways, Randall, Knight, Greening, Travers, H. Hansford, the Misses Lockwood and Mrs Edwin Randall (members of Loders Women's Institute), and Mr Edward Greening.

The band of the 224th Battery R.F.A., under Bandmaster Shepard, played selections throughout the afternoon and provided music for the dancing on the green with which the day's proceedings terminated.

Mr. F. Bartlett of the Crown, Loders (sic), supplied a refreshment tent.

The large marquee in which the exhibits were displayed presented a charming spectacle when the show was formally opened in the course of a brief speech by Mrs. Le Breton, who warmly congratulated both the Committee and the painstaking exhibitors..

A decorated wagon (left) probably from Upton Manor or Matravers Farm prior to the start of the parade.

The placard in the picture (above) refers to the Church bells. Loders Church bells were refurbished in 1927 so this was probably a fund raising event for the bells. The placard reads 'A Great Rally for the Church Bells, - A Splendid Procession - A Day of Delight at Loders'.

On the cart are Tom Hyde and Gwen (?). The man standing is Sidney Brown who lived at Locks Hill. He was the father of Harold who became Clerk to Loders Parish Council, a position he held for many years. He was the author of the book 'The Loders Book, A Village in a Dorset Valley'.

An Upton Manor Farm wagon with two magnificent horses decorated and led by Alec Peach and Jim Hawker. Both these men worked at Upton Manor Farm, a large employer in those days. This card was purchased from a Blandford dealer who 'claimed' it was a Loders card and he would take it back if not. My mother confirmed that indeed it was by saying "That's Uncle Alec and Uncle Jim!"

The same decorated wagon near the Forge in Uploders with Alec Peach on horseback and Jim Hawker walking by the side of the wagon.

The procession by Knowle Farm, Uploders. The wagon is from Brewers in Bridport, most likely Palmers.

The ladies from the Loders Women's Institute who ran the 1926 tea tent. (Standing) Sarah Ann Travers, Mrs Pitcher, Mrs Crabb, Mrs May Samways, Beatie Clark and Ethel Howe. (Seated) Mrs W Brown, Miss Lockwood, Mrs Fanny Greening, Mrs Jessie Hansford, Mrs Doris Randall and Mrs Knight.

Doris Randall (Harris) with the Hoop-la Stall. The sign reads 'One ball a penny, 7 for 6d' That's 7 balls for 2.5p in our decimal currency.

The entertainers (left to right) are:- Louise Hudson, Clara Ward, Bertha Symes (Young), Ruby Richards, Vera Knight (Tiltman), Ivy Coles, May Hudson, Lily Samways, Louise Paul, Dora Paul (Hyde), Linda Brown, Ivy Hansford, Doris Prior, Alice Rogers, Amy Symes (Metcalf), Doris Ward, Vera Legg and an unknown little girl hiding her face in her hands!

Mrs Hansford with Don Brown standing proudly beside his prize winning steam roller at the 1926 fête.

Ivy Read (Howard) and Violet Hyde in fancy dress as harlequins. They are both in the picture of the fête procession near Knowle Farm on page 132.

The First World War - Airships

During the 1914-18 War the Toller Admiralty Airship Sub-Station on Powerstock Common was one of three in the South West. Dirigibles from these undertook anti-submarine patrols over the Channel and escorted

(Above) An airship over The Trossachs (Butterwell) Uploders, heading towards the base at Powerstock. The picture was taken from the garden of Rose Cottage, just east of the Chapel, during or just after the 1914-18 War.

In the summer of 1917 a new airship flew from the main station at Mullion in Cornwall destined for Powerstock. It turned towards the coast near West Bay and according to a report in the Dorset County Magazine:-

Zero' passed low over a building painted with 'Bridport Laundry' on its roof when tall trees ripped off the starboard elevator. The crew released two bombs which did not explode, presumably in an endeavour to regain height, but its guy ropes caught in overhead telegraph cables causing it to veer to the left. It crashed into a hillside at Loders, narrowly missing a Sunday School party in a nearby field. All the airship fabric was ripped into fragments. A young girl, Emily Barnes from Loders Mill, brought goat's milk and cheese to the crashed airmen."

The airship crashed on Boarsbarrow Hill. There were no casualties. The only part of the airship to survive was its gondola (left) The pilot, John Owner, is foreground (left). There was no report of the crash in the local or national papers at the time, presumably because of wartime censorship.

The First World War

Many young men from Loders joined their peers to bravely fight for their King and Country during the 1914-18 War. Sadly many perished. Those from Loders who gave their lives are recorded on the Roll of Honour in Loders Church.

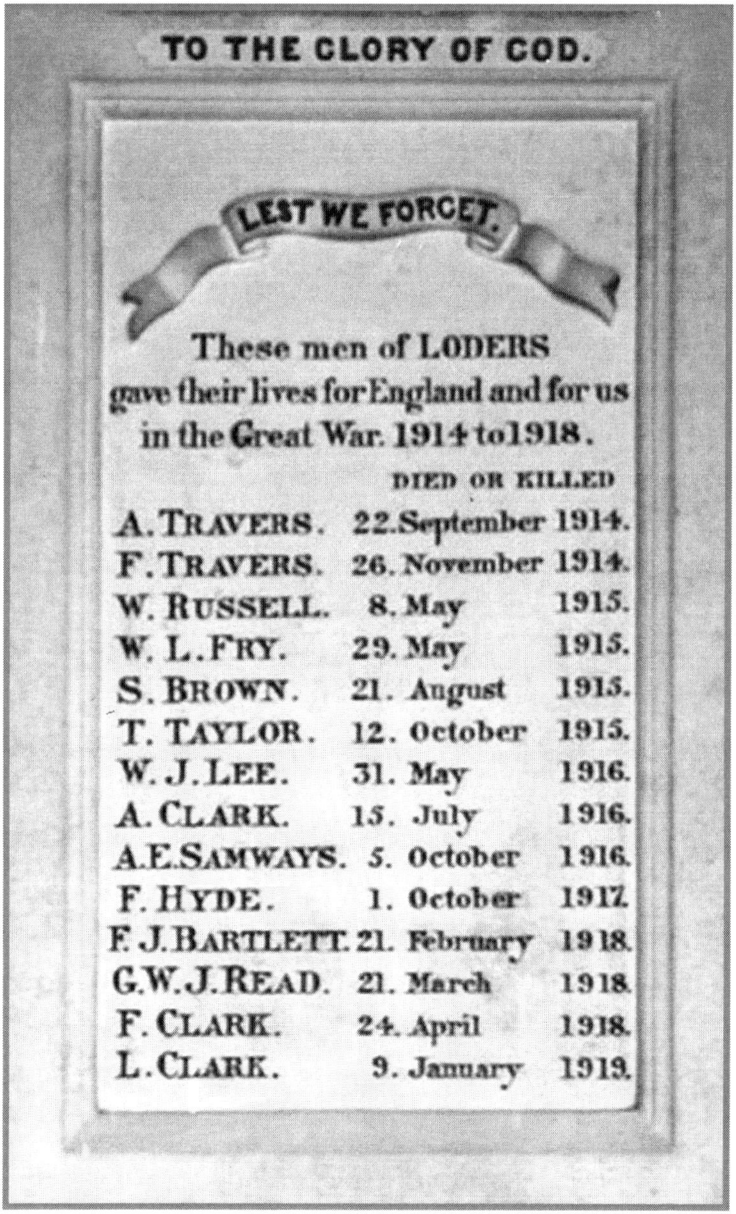

Memorial to the fallen of the First World War

The Second World War

1941, the Loders Home Guard under the command of Col Sir Edward Le Breton.
From the left, back row, Privates Ward, Legg, Paul, Tom Bourne, Percy Read, Saunders, Nobbs, Glyde, Darby and Darby.
Centre row, Privates Frank Osborne, Gurd, Reg Dennett, George Hyde, Fred Taylor, Walker, Ted Collier, George Crabb, Maurice Tucker, Harry Crabb.
Front row: - Cpl Jack Chester, Sgt Henry Tucker, Sgt A Budden, Capt G Wellstead, Col Sir Edward Le Breton, Sgt Albert Wells, Cpl Wrixon and Cpl Shelton.
Sitting cross-legged is Wilf Crabb, the Boy Scout and messenger for the troop.

When they became old enough some of the younger members of the Home Guard were called up to serve their Country. George Crabb was one. Other boys from the village also saw action and survived. Three, sadly, did not. Their names are on the Roll of Honour in Loders Church they are:

Tom Samuel Norman Born in 1919 he attended Loders School from September 1924 to January 1931. He was a Private in the Royal Army Ordnance Corps. Tom died on 1 March 1940, age 20. He is buried in Loders Cemetery.

George W C Holmes. Born in 1920 he attended Loders School from June 1925 to July 1934 He was an Aircraftsman 1st Class in the RAF. George died on war service on 14 April 1940 aged 19 at RAF Warmwell. He is buried in Loders Cemetery.

Frederick David Symes. Born at Uploders on 5 November 1917 he attended Loders School from 4 July 1921 to 31 July 1929 and then Bridport Grammar School. He joined the Royal Navy on 7th October 1940 and became a Signalman in the Royal Navy Patrol Service. David joined HMS Hebe on 31 August 1941 and was killed on active service on 22 November 1943 aged 26. His name is recorded on the Lowestoft Naval Memorial. There is a memorial to him in Loders Cemetery.

The Roadmen

This picture c1913, is thought to be on the A35 Dorchester to Bridport road near Travellers Rest. The men are loading stone from the heap at the roadside into the putt for filling potholes. The stone probably came from the quarry at the top of Stoney Head, near Knowl Lane. There were numerous quarries in the area usually with a nearby limekiln. From the left the men are George Read, George Marsh (the foreman, with the hat who is my great-grandfather), Mark Fooks and Eddie Fooks.

The gang, with the steam roller compacting the stone into the unsurfaced road. Fresh stone can be seen under the front wheel of the roller. The men are, from the left, Unknown, Unknown, George Read, Eddie Fooks, George Marsh, Mark Fooks and the unknown roller driver.

The Carriers

Poem Dedicated to Carrier, Mr Macey Recalled by Philip Symes

Why don't you leave my wife alone
She's so drunk she can't get home
We'll get old Macey's horse and cart
And bring her home when it's dark

In the early part of the 1900s the villagers relied on the local carriers with their horse or pony drawn wagons to transport goods to and from town. A small charge was made for deliveries and collections. The carriers picked up items the villagers wanted delivered and were given lists of items to be collected from the town. In the 1927 Kelley's Directory there are four carriers listed for the village: Sidney Ellis, J Macey & Son, Stephen Crabb, and Ernest Watts. All visited Bridport daily. Stephen Crabb also travelled to Weymouth on Fridays. Ernest John Watts, is also listed as a Motor car proprietor.

(Right) The carrier Mr Ellis outside of 3 Box Cottages where he lived. His sign is over the window.

The two lower pictures are enlargements from postcards which show carriers delivering to Lower Loders in the early 1900s.

Delivering to the Loders Arms (above) and two wagons near the Farmers Arms and Mr Budden's shop (right).

The Carriers and their Motor Vehicles

Steven Crabb's bus outside Brook Barton in Uploders where he lived and ran his business. Mr Crabb began with a horse and wagon and later acquired a bus. The destination on the front is 'Askerswell' which was on the end of his Bridport to Loders to Askerswell route which would have included a stop at Bridport Station. He also made butter and cheese on the premises. The little girl is thought to be his daughter Mabel Alice Crabb.

Ernest Watts's taxi business was based at Church Farm, Loders. His taxi service gave the locals much better and quicker journeys to town and connections to the railway station. In this picture he is about to set out for a local wedding. It was taken in March 1924; no publisher details given.

Deliveries

Up to the Second World War the village had its own tradesmen, small shops, carriers and farms to provide produce and services. Most of the workers were employed in the village, or nearby.

The Baker, Fred Marsh, at Hembury Mill, Askerswell where the corn was milled and the bread baked. It was delivered to Askerswell, Shipton Gorge and Uploders. There was no baker in Loders. In the late 1900s the last descendant of the Marsh family at Hembury Mill passed away. The mill has now been restored and remains a monument to times gone by.

In the 1920s and before, milk from the farms was sold direct to the villagers. It was either collected from the farms or delivered.

(Right) Annie Foot carries milk around the village in two pails hung from a yolk. The milk was ladled into jugs and containers at her customers' houses.

Deliveries from The Grocery Man

As well as the fetching and carrying provided by the carriers some grocery shops in Bridport delivered to customers in and around the town.

One of the grocery firms that delivered to Loders was Elliott's. This picture, taken c1930, shows Elliott's shop when it was located next to the hotel, The King of the Belgians, previously The King of Prussia and now The Lord Nelson. Elliot's later moved next door to the Bull Hotel, the premises now occupied by Bridget's, the fruit and vegetable shop.

Also in the picture are Elliott's delivery van and the staff who are, from left to right, Harry Sprake, Jack Tuck, Len Read, Joe Jeanes, Mr Norris, George Elliott (the owner), Marjorie Hawkins and Mr Symes.

Joe Jeanes drove the van and was responsible for taking the customers' orders and delivering their groceries. He had regular rounds so would call on his customers the same day each week with his notebook and pencil to take the order for that week. He delivered the order a day or two later.

In a way it was not unlike the internet ordering of today. But it was a personal service provided by local firms employing local people to people they knew.

Braiding

It was unusual for women to return to work after starting a family. Many in and around Bridport were employed as outworkers by the local net factories. The work was sometimes heavy, often dusty and the pay poor. But it was an opportunity to earn extra money. The braiders provided the needles and laces needed to make the nets. These were usually home-made and branded with the braider's own particular mark.

Mrs Martha Crabb braiding nets at the table in her cottage next to Loders School. This picture was used for the calendar for W Edwards & Son (Bridport) Ltd: net, line and twine manufacturers.

Tables used for braiding became worn with deep grooves from the continuous rubbing of the nets against the table top and legs.

Mrs Crabb was a great favourite with the school children next door. She chatted over her garden wall and returned any wayward balls with a smile.

(Right) Mrs Ellis, the wife of the carrier, on the steps of 3 Box Cottages, Uploders.

In the summer months the women often worked outside. They had the benefit of the fresh air and no dust from the twine in their houses.

Two tools were needed; a needle to hold the twine and a lace to create the mesh. The lace was circular in section and about 6 inches long. It had to be of the exact diameter for the mesh size. Each braider had a selection of needles and laces for every type of net they might encounter.

Braiding for the War Effort - War-time pictures

Twine delivered to Hilda Greening by delivery-man Fred Symes. He called on fixed days, usually once or twice a week depending on the urgency of the work. He booked-out the twine, collected the finished nets and made payment in cash.

Sylvia Hyde, Martha Crabb, Adelaide Hyde, Lizzie Crabb and Sis Gale braiding large mesh nets probably camouflage nets, outside Box Cottages in Uploders.

Rose Cottage 1941: The Crabb and Symes children who were cousins supporting the war effort and their mothers by filling needles ready for braiding camouflage nets. They are, from the left, Ernest Crabb, Rodney Symes, Ann Crabb, Mrs Emily Symes, Philip Symes, Wilfred Crabb and Oscar Symes. Just to the right of Mrs Symes is the 'Swift'. This held the twine and rotated as the needles were filled.

Needles, laces and twine used by my grandmother and mother. The owner's mark, usually a letter, was burnt on using a hot iron. Small needles were used for small mesh nets and the very large ones for cargo nets on aircraft. Needles and laces were all handmade, usually by the man of the house. Synthetic twine replaced the natural fibres in the 1960s. It was smoother and less dusty but not so good for gardening purposes. The villagers were never short of twine!

Braiding - National Coverage

Just occasionally the local people were the subject of national interest. On 7 November 1971 an article appeared in the Sunday Times about nets and netmaking in the Bridport area featuring Elizabeth (Lizzie) Crabb who lived in Rose Cottage, a lovely thatched house in Uploders. Mrs Crabb was one of many of the women in and around Bridport whose earnings supplemented those of her working husband.

Lizzie braiding at her spotless scrubbed table which had been moved outside on a warm summer day. The onions hanging on the wall to dry were, no doubt, from the garden and grown and tended by husband Harry.

(Below) Lizzie in Rose Cottage working on heavy aircraft cargo nets. Although these were heavy, the thick nylon cord was clean and fairly easy to handle. In small cottages the large nets were cumbersome and conspicuous. However, the rate of pay was much better than for light small mesh nets.

Braiding in Loders by Fra. H Newbery

This print of Braiding in Loders by Fra Newbery is based on one of the four panel murals in Bridport Town Hall. According to Newbery's notes it's Myrtle Cottage, Loders, the home of Alice Bagg. There is a Myrtle Cottage in Uploders but when Newbery painted this picture, that was known as Temperance Cottage. On the Electoral Registers throughout the 1920s Mr and Mrs Macey (of Macey's corner fame) are shown as living in Myrtle Cottage. This identifies the property visited by Newbery as the house known as Raikes. The view of the Church through the doorway must be artistic licence but is totally acceptable.

Fra Newbery, was Director of the Glasgow School of Art between 1885 and 1918. It was Newbery who commissioned Rennie Mackintosh to redesign the Campus. Fra Newbery remains an important name in the art world and is well known in Bridport where his career began. He retired to Corfe Castle in 1918. During his retirement he painted several pictures depicting Bridport's history and trade. In 1925 the Town Hall was redecorated to his design, including the four-panelled mural, one panel of which shows this picture.

Fra Newbery's daughter married into the Nesbitt family of Philadelphia. His grand -daughter died in about 2005 in the US and it seems that her daughter, Newbery's great-granddaughter, attached little importance to any old papers, prints and photographs that originated from him. Luckily a dealer in the USA did and rescued some of the material and sold what he could on eBay. The prints included copies of the murals in the Town Hall. The prints were produced by Newbery. On the fronts he signed them and gave the locations (see below). On the back he wrote, *"To his Brother Tom from the Artist. Corfe Castle, Dorset, Sept/29".*

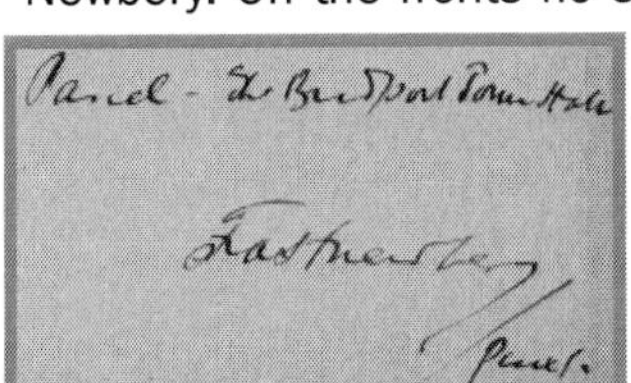

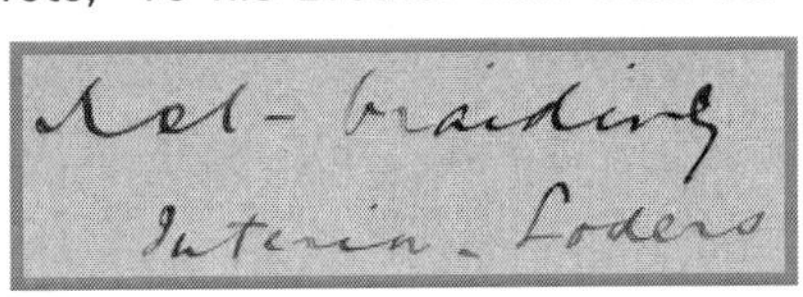

Hygiene and Beauty

Emily Symes washing the hair of two of her children, Phyllis and Mabel at the communal pump which provided water for 1, 2 and 3 Box Cottages and Garden Cottage. Tom Bartlett, retired blacksmith, watches the fun from his back door.

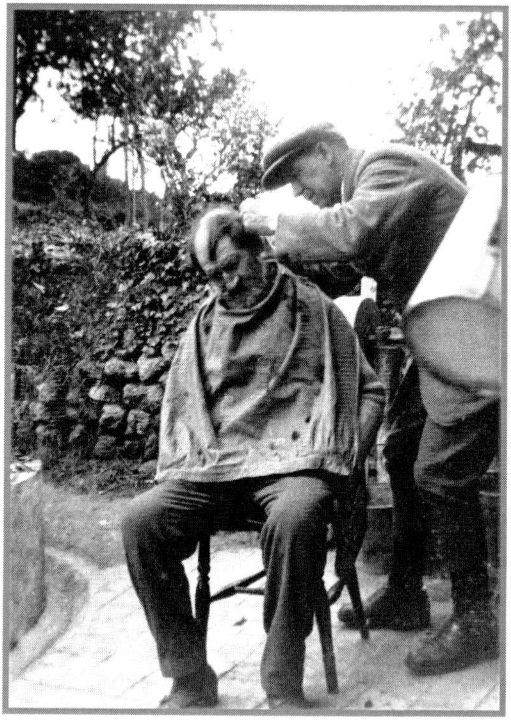

There was no barber's shop in the village. Instead the part-time travelling barber Fred Collier, visited his customers. Here he is giving Oscar Gale a trim outside the back door of Rose Cottage.

Fred travelled around the village on a bicycle with a box over the back wheel to carry his gear. In his later years he was hardly ever seen riding his bicycle. He just walked beside it.

Leisure Activities

Although life in the village was hard there was always time for leisure and play.

An Outing to Weymouth in 1921

A trip to Weymouth in a Bonfield & Son of Bridport Renault charabanc. Clearly the weather was good but how did those hats stay on during the journey? From the right the passengers are:- Charlie Crabb, George Crabb, ?....?, Ivy Collier (May), Ethel Howe, Enid Crabb (Crabb), Elsie Read, Mabel Williams, ?....?, Amy Symes (Metcalf), Doris Legg, ?....?, ?....?, Ned Eveleigh, J. Eveleigh, ?....?, and the driver (and village carrier) Steven Crabb and his family,

A crowd watching the hunt meet outside Loders School. Among the riders is Harold Bishop from Yondover Farm on the horse third from left. As women make up most of the crowd, it is likely that the meet was on a weekday when most of the men were at work.

The Loders Women's Institute

Based on reports in the Bridport News the Loders WI was active between 1919 and 1940 as well as post World War II.

Bridport News 14 November 1919

WOMEN'S INSTITUTE SOCIAL.– To augment the fund for purchasing a piano for the Institute, a social was recently held. A good programme of songs, &c., was gone through, after which the room was cleared for dancing.

Loders WI at Loders Court c1935. Centre-front is Lady Le Breton. All but three of the ladies are in smart hats and look rather grand.

Bridport News 27 September 1940

The Women's Institute met at the Parish Room on Thursday, Mrs Lesser presiding. Sympathetic reference was made by Mrs Le Breton to the death of Mrs Greening, the oldest member, and all stood in silence. A letter was read from the County Treasurer gratefully acknowledging the Institute's donation of £2 6s to the Red Cross ambulance. Mr Lesser, A.R.P. warden, gave an interesting talk on A.R.P. work, with some valuable advice on what to do in an air raid or in a possible attack by gas. It was unanimously decided that after the October meeting (at which a war-time cookery demonstration will be given by Miss White) the general meeting should be suspended during the winter months and resumed again in the spring.

Meetings ceased some time during the Second World War. With the suspension agreed at the 27 September 1940 meeting it is a fair assumption that the break extended to 1947 when the WI became active once again. Its 'new' 10th birthday was reported in the July 1957 edition of the Reverend Willmott's Parish Notes. The August 1957 edition contained the correction as quoted below.

The comment of our most distinguished reader on the paragraph last month about the W.I. celebrating their tenth birthday was: "Tenth birthday my foot! Feminine Vanity! They must be at least forty". And so, we suppose, they are, if they be dated from when they begun. The ladies prefer to date themselves from when they revived.

The Loders Scouts in 1924 and 1941

The Scouts in 1924, when they won the final of the District Boy Scouts competition and so qualified for the County finals. The winning team was Patrol Leaders Wilfred Hansford and George Hicks, Seconds Harold Saunders and Edward Crabb and Scouts Frank Crabb and Elston Paul. No doubt they are in the picture with Sir Edward Le Breton who is seated centre in the middle row.

The Loders Scouts in 1941, including boys from Bradpole and evacuees.
Sir Edward Le Breton was a keen scouter and bought the uniforms for the troop.
(Back from left) Vic Mears, -?-, Horace Read, Ron Churchill, ? Hyde, Oscar Symes, Peter Rogers, Philip Symes, Peter Lee, Dennis Yarde.
(Front Row) Clifford Pitcher, ? Galpin, Dennis Chilcott, ? Galpin, Scout Leader Jim Cranston, Ted Guppy, Geoff Guppy, -?-, Wilf Crabb.

The Loders Ladies' Football Team in the mid-1920s

In a close fought match the Loders Ladies had a 4-3 win against the Powerstock Ladies on 2 January in a charity match to raise money for the blind. Back row far right, is Nellie Hansford (Crabb) Jessie's mother and front second from the left, is Ena Crabb (Crabb), Maureen's mother.

The Loders Mothers' Union in the 1930s

The Mothers' Union on a sunny afternoon at Loders Court. Lady Le Breton is sitting at the front, fourth from the right, with her dog. Behind and to her left is Lizzie Hyde. Sitting on the pillar (third left) is Agnes Hansford.

The Lost Public Houses - The Blue Ball

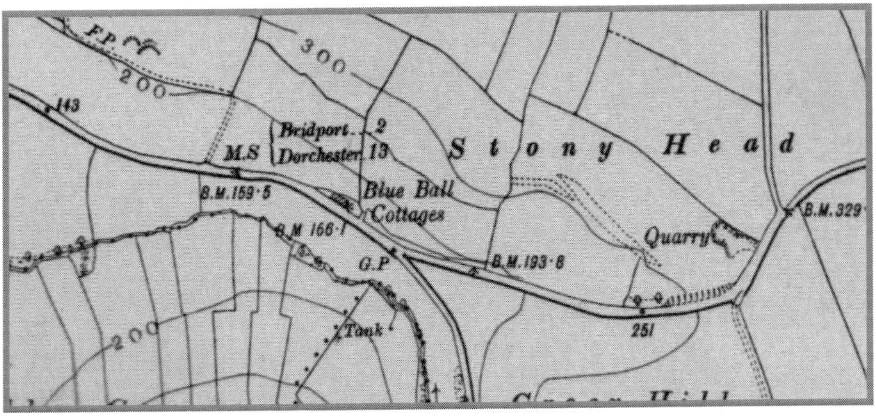

Blue Ball Cottages were located on the A35 at the bottom of the steep hill and narrow cutting at Stoney Head. This extract from the 1930 Ordnance Survey Six-inch to One-mile map shows the cottages on the old turnpike road, now the A35 trunk road, close to the junction to Shipton Gorge. The Blue Ball Inn was recorded on the 1871 Census. Steven Ackerman was the landlord. The cottages had no well and water was collected from over the road which was not so busy then.

The cottages were demolished in 1972 when the A35 was realigned. They were used as site offices for the Contractor and Resident Engineer during the works. I spent several months there supervising the works but did not take a photograph of the cottages. Luckily Philip Symes did. The cottages were at the bottom of the hill where a few vehicles are parked. An attractive rambling rose with small red double flowers grew at the front of the cottages. I took a cutting which rooted and thrived in our garden in Dorchester. From reports received soon after we left in 1994 it no longer exists. I really should have taken another cutting!

Vinney Cross — Once a Beer-house?

Searching various Directories and censuses to find when the Blue Ball ceased to be an Inn I noticed reference to Vinney Cross. In the 1841 Census Mathew Gill, the head of house, was listed as an Inn-keeper. The Hunt & Co. Dorset Directory 1851 lists him as a Beer Retailer but there is no mention of this in the 1851 census when Ellen Gill, his daughter and net braider, was the sole occupant of the house. Around 1841 for a few years, it seems, it was a simply a beer-house.

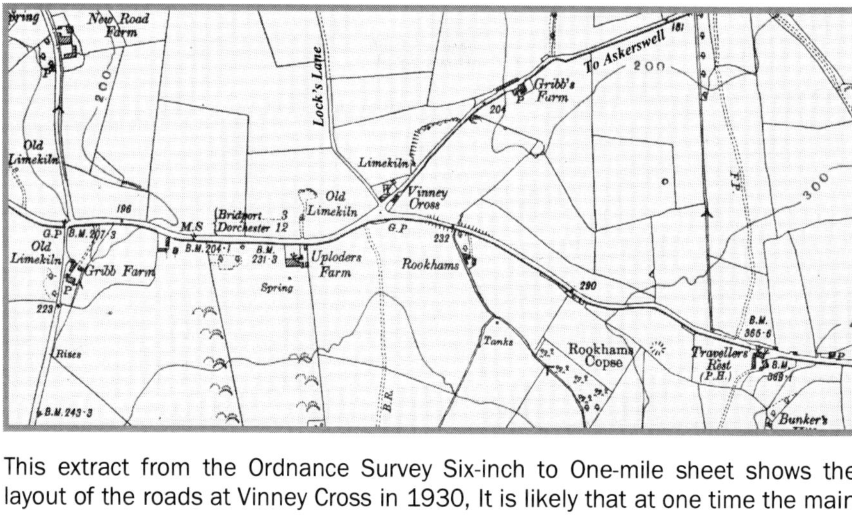

This extract from the Ordnance Survey Six-inch to One-mile sheet shows the layout of the roads at Vinney Cross in 1930, It is likely that at one time the main route was from Bridport towards Askerswell and Eggardon with Lock's Lane (the lane going northwards from the cross) and the Dorchester roads being the roads of lesser importance. A beer-house at Vinney Cross would have tempted those travellers who would not be passing the Travellers Rest.

The Travellers Rest and Rabbiting

Travellers Rest on the A35 is sometimes thought to be in Shipton Gorge or Askerswell but it's actually in Loders close to the eastern boundary of the parish. It ceased to be a public house in the 1980s. Ron Foot was the final landlord.

A very successful rabbiting party near the Travellers Rest. Rabbits were a pest. Hunting them helped the farmers and provided welcome meals for the villagers. The man in the centre with the trilby hat and looking full of importance is a Mr Hansford. The rabbits have been paunched (gutted) and their back legs split and joined to be carried on a pole. The dogs no doubt had a good morning and the flagons of cider along with the food basket made sure the men were kept suitably nourished and refreshed.

Bell - The Inn and the Lime Kiln

The first recorded licence for Bell was in 1749. The 1841 and 1851 censuses and the 1855 and 1859 Kelly's Directories record Thomas Hyde as Innkeeper. In the 1861 Census he was listed as a market gardener. The Inn had closed. During the construction of the Bridport to Maiden Newton Railway (1855-1857) it was a lodging place for construction workers. According to Hilda Greening, it lost its licence due to 'rowdy' behaviour of the workers on Saturday nights. They had money in their pockets. What else was there at Bell in the way of entertainment?

The lime kiln at Bell is one of several once found in the village. Others were located at Loders Cross, Gribb Farm, Green Hill (south of Stoney Head), Callington (Perwin Farm), Vinney Cross and Upton Farm. The kilns were always built alongside limestone quarries. Lime for soil improvement was produced by burning the excavated rock. The lime was also used in the production of mortar, whitewash and plaster.

Hole House Farm, Almost Journey's End

One final reminiscence, Hole House farm (on the right) was a place I visited with my mother and father for eggs and a chat with the farmer, Jack Dare and his wife. Jack always had a barrel, or two, of cider in the barn on the left as you passed through on the way to the back of the house. Jack sometimes offered my father a tipple and if he accepted Jack would say, "Would the b'woy like a drop?" to which the reply was, "He's not old enough yet".

Eventually I was old enough so Jack picked up one of the glass tankards from alongside the barrel. Like the others it looked as if it had never been washed. It was stained brown from cider and covered in bits of straw and dust. Jack turned it upside-down and shook out the debris, took it to the barrel, turned on the tap and part-filled it with the slightly cloudy liquid and passed it to me. I inspected it carefully and rather squeamishly. I wondered who had last drunk out of it and tried to ignore the bits floating on the top. I took a sip, it almost took the lining off my mouth but when it slipped down I felt a warm and pleasant glow. I had no problem knocking it all back and eagerly looked forward to my next visit!

Approaching Bradpole and Journey's End

Having travelled the length of Loders through Uploders, Yondover and Lower Loders we reach Hole House Farm (above right) and the sight of the Bradpole Church spire. Just around the corner is the Mangerton River and Bradpole. The carrier in this picture, c1905, would have shared the same journey many, many times on his trips to Bridport and around.

This bridge carries the road from Loders over the Mangerton River to Bradpole and places beyond. The parish boundary follows the centre of the river. Bradpole is on the left, Loders on the right. To the inhabitants of Loders it's Bradpole Bridge but John Giles-Townsend, a resident of Bradpole for over 80 years, told me that to the people of Bradpole it's Loders Bridge. Depending on which side of the river you live either name makes sense but to me and the people of Loders it's Bradpole Bridge; final word and no argument, and its where our journey ends.

Bibliography

The Loders Book - A Village in a Dorset Valley by S.H. Brown

Loders - The Priory, The Church and The Manor by Sir Edward Le Breton

A Walk Through Long Loders by Pat Hughes, Illustrated by Barry Wilson

Yours Reverently from the Parish Notes 1948-53 by the Reverend Oliver Willmott

The Parson Knows from the Parish Notes 1953-1968 by the Reverend Oliver Willmott

Various Documents - The Loders History Society

The Bridport Railway by B.L. Jackson and M.J. Tattershall

Powerstock Station - All Change by Diana P Read

The Bridport News

The Western Gazette

The Sunday Times

The Marshwood Vale Magazine

The Dorset County Magazine

Kelly's Directory of Dorsetshire (Various editions)

The Hunt & Co. Dorset Directory 1851

Ordnance Survey Maps - Various Old Editions

The Author

Bernard Paull grew up in Uploders. He attended Loders School from the age of five, moving to Bridport Grammar School aged eleven. A year later, in 1956, the three secondary schools in Bridport combined to become the Alfred Colfox School, one of the first comprehensives in Dorset. Following his success in Maths, Physics and Chemistry at 'A' level he was accepted for a position of Trainee Engineer in the County Surveyor's Department of Dorset County Council (DCC). This involved three years study at Plymouth College of Technology (now Plymouth University) leading to a University of London External Degree in Civil Engineering; BSc.(Eng.).

Following several years of experience in highway and bridge design and site supervision he qualified as a Chartered Engineer with both the Institution of Municipal Engineers and the Institution of Civil Engineers (ICE). He worked for DCC for 35 years reaching the level of Chief Engineer in the Consultancy arm of the Transportation and Engineering Department. He was a committee member with the Devon, Somerset and Dorset branch of the ICE and Secretary for a number of years.

At Local Government reorganisation in 1997 he joined Bridport Town Council as Town Surveyor where he remained until retiring in 2007. He served on the Friends of Bridport Museum committee and the Bridport Millennium Green Trust.

Bernard is a keen stamp and postcard collector and member of the Bridport and District Stamp and Postcard Club, Polonus (the Polish Philatelic Society in the US) and the Polish Philatelic Society in GB. He has had articles published in the latter's society magazine.

He is a trustee and treasurer for the Loders Village Hall Management Committee. He enjoys his garden and allotment which provide a plentiful supply of fresh fruit, vegetables and flowers to family and friends as well as good exercise for him!

On retirement he was invited to join the Rotary Club of Bridport where he met a group of like-minded people helping worthy causes and supporting the community. He was Club Secretary for about five years and President in 2017/18, the Club's 70th Anniversary year.

He is married to Christine. They have two daughters, Julia an accountant and Helen an architect. Their two granddaughters Abigail and Francesca Lincoln both went to Loders School and are now doing well at the Sir John Colfox Academy.